YOUR UNSTOPPABLE GREATNESS

Break Free from Impostor Syndrome, Cultivate Your Agency, and Achieve Your Ultimate Career Goals

Lisa Orbé-Austin, PhD
and Richard Orbé-Austin, PhD

ULYSSES PRESS

Published by:
Ulysses Press
PO Box 3440
Berkeley, CA 94703
www.ulyssespress.com

ISBN: 978-1-64604-407-8
Library of Congress Control Number: 2022936256

Printed in the United States by Versa Press
10 9 8 7 6 5 4 3 2 1

Acquisitions editor: Bridget Thoreson
Managing editor: Claire Chun
Project editor: Renee Rutledge
Editor: Kirsten Janene-Nelson
Front cover design: Ashley Prine
Cover art: © djero.adlibeshe yahoo.com/shutterstock.com
Interior art: chapter and part start pages © Vandathai/shutterstock.com; pages 108, 120 © Kiyan Fox; page 108 people © Sube29/shutterstock.com; page 108 hand © yut548/shutterstock.com; page 120 graphics © Leremy/shutterstock.com
Production: Winnie Liu

IMPORTANT NOTE TO READERS: This book has been written and published for informational and educational purposes only. It is not intended to serve as medical advice or to be any form of medical treatment. You should always consult with your physician before altering or changing any aspect of your medical treatment. Do not stop or change any prescription medications without the guidance and advice of your physician. Any use of the information in this book is made on the reader's good judgment and is the reader's sole responsibility. This book is not intended to diagnose or treat any medical condition and is not a substitute for a physician. This book is independently authored and published, and no sponsorship or endorsement of this book by, and no affiliation with, any trademarked brands or other products mentioned within is claimed or suggested. All trademarks that appear in this book belong to their respective owners and are used here for informational purposes only. The authors and publisher encourage readers to patronize the brands mentioned in this book.

CONTENTS

Chapter 9
CONQUERING LEADERSHIP PITFALLS 140

Chapter 10
DEVELOPING HEALTHY LEADERSHIP 158

CONCLUSION: YOUR UNSTOPPABLE GREATNESS 169

NOTES 171

ACKNOWLEDGMENTS 175

ABOUT THE AUTHORS 176

INTRODUCTION

In the time since we released our first book, *Own Your Greatness: Overcome Impostor Syndrome, Beat Self-Doubt, and Succeed in Life,* we have gotten to witness up close so many people transforming from the paralysis of the impostor cycle to the freedom of embracing their competencies, skills, abilities, experiences, and, most importantly, their dreams. We've seen the people who worked through the book do remarkable things: double their salaries; advocate for and receive the promotion they'd been waiting for; courageously change careers and start businesses; give TEDx talks; cut their work hours and spend more valuable time on their own and with their loved ones; obtain their dream jobs at their dream companies; get their first C-suite roles; and—overall—just blossom, grow, expand, and live in their greatness. Learning about these successes has been the most beautiful and special gift—especially since much of it occurred during the grim time of the COVID-19 pandemic. This experience teaching people how to use the skills, tools, and concepts of the 3C's (Clarify, Choose, and Create) Strategy to break their impostor syndrome has been for us a brilliant light in the darkness. We look forward to seeing and hearing about more transformations as people continue to find and use *Own Your Greatness* to finally face the impostor syndrome beast.

As we've helped people transform in our master class; in trainings at their companies, associations, and universities; and through our individual coaching work, we've experienced firsthand that it's possible for people to learn these skills in a short period of time. We also saw something very interesting that led us to writing *this* book.

We saw amazing professionals—who had done the hard work of addressing their underlying issues and building tools using the model of the first book—finally believe in themselves in completely new and powerful ways. Nevertheless, we also saw them sometimes being dragged back—kicking and screaming—to places of insecurity and overwork by work cultures that were unrelentingly intent on getting the result they wanted from their employees. Witnessing these struggles fortified our passion for addressing and tackling the societal and work culture issues that reinforce both impostor syndrome and the mechanisms and types of leadership models that sustain it within these organizations. We want to make the invisible forcefield of toxicity transparent so that you can, first, identify it and then either address it or make other choices about whether you will invest your skills and talents in it.

In this book, we want to discuss the agency you feel you have (or don't have) within an organization/system—and what you can do to make sure you're empowered, even in very difficult situations. One difficulty many experience derives from how, when we think about systemic issues, we often have trouble identifying who is at the center and whom we can hold accountable. That scenario is what can be referred to as trying to "kiss the system"—which of course is impossible. We want to help you embrace the understanding that it's *individuals* who make up the systems and create the policies, procedures, and cultures that are toxic. We want to help you examine the ways toxic systems may be pulling on you to revert to the old habits of impostor syndrome. Through your experience with this book, we want you to reexamine your relationship with work, with your workplace, and with its leadership. We want you to make conscious choices about who you are in these circumstances, how you relate to others, and how to deal with difficult situations. We often say that we don't want you to play checkers when everyone else is playing chess. We want to teach you how to be a chess master by being intentional about your moves, by understanding the players and what your ultimate goal is, and by having a plan about how you're going to achieve that goal—even in the most difficult of situations.

THE 3 A'S MODEL FOR REACHING YOUR UNSTOPPABLE GREATNESS: AGENCY, ASSESSMENT, AND ACTUALIZATION

In Part One—Chapters 1 through 3, we'll look at the agency you've developed thus far (perhaps from working on your impostor syndrome in *Own Your Greatness*), and we'll help you to use it to strategically reimagine your dreams for your future—or, perhaps, to dream them for the first time. We'll also challenge you to consider ways you can protect your dreams until you can make them happen.

Part Two—Chapters 4 through 7—is about assessment. We'll help you think about how you relate to systems and organizations—and how you can redefine that relationship as you move away from relying on systems for validation of your competency, skills, and experience. We want you to instead consider how to interact with these systems in a way that's beneficial and healthy for *you*. A significant part of this process is learning to identify and evaluate toxic systems, leaders, and work cultures—and then to assess how to engage those systems while also protecting yourself. We'll also discuss how systems of oppression benefit and reinforce impostor syndrome. Then we'll explore how you can empower and believe in yourself even from within oppressive systems—all while working to eradicate them.

In Part Three—Chapters 8 through 10—we'll discuss how to be an agent of change using the competencies essential to developing cultures that don't reinforce impostor syndrome. Even if you are not yet a formal leader, it's important to consider your influence and the ways you can support environments that will be healthier for yourself and others. It is essential to understand that leadership—and the way you interact with, develop, support, and model for your team—is meaningful, especially in how that leadership creates ripple effects in the system. Just one person can disrupt a system if that person builds a community to help create an alternative culture, one meant to nurture and value the most important asset to any organization—its people!

Throughout the book, hypothetical case studies are provided for illustrative purposes only and do not represent an actual client or an actual client's experience, but rather are meant to provide an example of the process and methodology of the book. An individual's experience may vary based on their individual circumstances. There can be no assurance that everyone will be able to achieve similar results in comparable situations. No portion of this book is to be interpreted as testimonial or endorsement of our services.

If you read and completed *Own Your Greatness,* you'll know that book is a primer for developing the skills called for in this book. We want to help you develop skills and tools to exercise your agency and continue to challenge impostor syndrome, even in complex situations and cultures. We want you to engage with this book. Complete the exercises, take time to reflect. THIS IS WORK, and IT WORKS! And that work is worth it. You won't regret the time you spend on it.

Welcome to this journey! We're happy to be here with you.

PART ONE
AGENCY

Chapter 1

(RE)ENVISIONING THE DREAM

In 2020 we gave a TEDx talk called "The Impostor Syndrome Paradox: Unleashing the Power of You."[1] In it, Lisa shared how she'd had a toxic job that inflamed and reinforced her impostor syndrome—and so she resigned.

CASE STUDY: LISA

When Lisa quit that job, she was spinning. It felt like her whole world went into chaos. She was actively questioning everything she'd thought she was going to do with her career. As she slowly came out of the shock, some dreams that she'd buried started to resurface. Dreams that others around her had told her were "unrealistic" or "wouldn't make an impact." She had allowed herself to be swayed by those opinions, which she had considered more valid than her own. She had wanted those people to be proud of her, and to feel that she valued their opinions. Plus, she just trusted their views over her own. But as she was coming out of the fog of decades of impostor syndrome, she felt more and more certain that nobody (or very few people) knew her better than she knew herself—and that she needed to start connecting with what she wanted and needed if she was going to be happy with the choices she made.

Many people who have worked through *Own Your Greatness* have told us they feel like a veil has been lifted, like they can see the world with new eyes. The beauty of that is people start to *really* own their greatness and see the power of that—by asking for raises and promotions, starting the businesses they always wanted, and setting boundaries in ways they never thought possible. The immense possibilities that surface as a part of this awakening can be so exciting, even breathtaking.

However, there is another side to this amazing moment of revelation. When you've spent a significant period of your life searching for external validation—indeed, relying on it to help you determine both the big and small steps to take next—you can be left questioning whether you're in the right workplace, or even the right career path. Have you kept your own intentions and hopes at the forefront of your decisions? Even if you're clear you're in the right place, it can still be very disorienting to consider that maybe your dreams were too small and constricted, or maybe you relied too much on what *others* would be proud of.

In this first chapter, we want to start with revisioning your dreams. All too often those of us who experience impostor syndrome find our dreams are hidden, or even nonexistent. We want to begin with you—with what you want for yourself—and to center that as you proceed through this book.

BREAKING THE IMPOSTOR SYNDROME CYCLE

You likely know that impostor syndrome doesn't occur all the time; it occurs when you're triggered. Some of the most common triggers are new work projects with some vulnerability, say because you haven't mastered the task yet, or you feel rusty and not at the top of your game; or complex projects with lots of room for error; or highly visible events like public speaking or presenting to senior leaders or important stakeholders. There's an additional set of triggers if you're part of a historically marginalized group—if you're a woman, a person of color, an immigrant, etc.—especially when that group has been stereotyped and discriminated against and seen as less than: less capable, less intelligent, less competent. Impostor syndrome can be triggered by incidents of discrimination, microaggression, isolation, lack of mentorship, and inequitable treatment and access. Another culprit is "gaslighting," which refers to a situation where, say, you're being treated poorly because you're a woman in a male-dominated environment—but someone claims you're mistaken, telling you it's "all in your head."

Everyone—all genders and gender expressions—can experience impostor syndrome. Research tells us that we all experience it differently, and with different degrees of frequency. Women may experience it more because they may exhibit more "counterphobic" behavior—meaning they may lean *in* to the fear, and so they may be triggered more often. Some men may be triggered less if they avoid taking risks that could expose them as a fraud. In *Own Your Greatness*, we emphasize the value of knowing our triggers and provide exercises for identifying them;

armed with that understanding, we can pause and consciously choose different behaviors. For example, instead of overworking, we can practice time- and project-management; instead of self-sabotaging, we can break large tasks into manageable ones—and thus manage our performance anxiety as well. What's more, we can break the cycle at any point, and we can manage performance anxiety with mindfulness exercises. With practice, we can learn to accept and internalize the positive feedback we get for walking our path—and learn how to properly address any critical feedback we get, without overfocusing on it. Learning how to break the impostor cycle is central to the skills we'll use so as to live our dreams.

EXERCISE 1.1: ASSESSING YOUR SKILLS IN BREAKING THE IMPOSTOR SYNDROME CYCLE

Think about your process of cycle-breaking. Consider your strengths: What are you consistently good at identifying and addressing? What are you still struggling with? The different cycle-breaking skills are listed in the left column of the table below. For each skill, identify if you feel you've mastered it or if it's still a work in progress.

Skills in Breaking the Impostor Syndrome Cycle	SKILLED	DEVELOPING
Identifying triggers	☐	☐
Pausing and choosing optimal behaviors (e.g., internalizing positive feedback, project managing, setting boundaries, etc.)	☐	☐
Managing performance anxiety	☐	☐
Addressing overworking	☐	☐
Monitoring self-sabotage (e.g., practicing time management and mindfulness instead of procrastinating)	☐	☐
Internalizing positive feedback	☐	☐
Handling negative/critical feedback	☐	☐

Now, consider how you can address the cycle-breaking skills you're still developing.

SKILLS I'M DEVELOPING	DIFFICULTIES I'VE ENCOUNTERED	MY NEXT STEPS IN IMPROVING THIS SKILL

As you can imagine, since new experiences can specifically trigger impostor syndrome, learning how to break the cycle is fundamental to conquering it.

REASSESSING ORGANIZATIONAL LOYALTY

Additionally, sometimes impostor syndrome correlates to other factors that discourage us from constructing new dreams. If we don't feel we (fully) deserve our position in an organization, we might feel particularly indebted and loyal to it—even if it's not as loyal or committed to us—and so we might remain there longer than really serves us. Also, if we lack knowledge about the job market, we might assume we have no other options. And job searches are onerous: we don't want our résumés scrutinized or our inadequacy discovered in an interview. The problem is job security turns out to be merely an illusion when our insurance plan is changed or we get laid off. As we move away from the concepts of codependence that underlie impostor syndrome, we need to move toward thoughts of creating our *own* security—through our skills, credentials, decisions, and experience. Because, ultimately, an employer only compensates us for the work that we do for their organization. They do not provide us guaranteed security—we create and guarantee security for ourselves.

It's important to break this mentality of organizational loyalty because it prevents us from relying on systems that, though healthy at times, can also be toxic. Orienting toward autonomy is particularly key for those struggling with impostor syndrome because it enables us to take a healthier stance when evaluating whether we're being adequately compensated or valued for the work we contribute—whereas if we focus on the real or imagined security the company provides, we'll typically overestimate the security and undervalue our compensation and treatment.

As we discuss in *Own Your Greatness*, impostor syndrome often derives from codependent and narcissistic family dynamics in our childhood; unfortunately, these dynamics are often replicated in our workplaces. Those who've worked through our first book have worked to break away from these dynamics, both personally and with individuals, perhaps with the help of a therapist. It's now time to do that work in an organizational setting by engaging with the following exercises.

EXERCISE 1.2: RECOGNIZING CODEPENDENT DYNAMICS IN A WORK SETTING

Ask yourself if you identify with the following questions—checking "yes" or "no" for each.

Your Behaviors	YES	NO
Are you particularly focused on pleasing your boss?	☐	☐
Do you struggle to set boundaries out of concern that others will be upset with you?	☐	☐
Do you have difficulty sharing an opinion contrary to that of others?	☐	☐
Do you feel that getting the job done is more important than your need to take care of yourself?	☐	☐
Do you have a hard time assessing if you're doing a good job without someone else telling you?	☐	☐
Are you concerned about the team liking you (especially when giving difficult feedback or offering a contradictory position)?	☐	☐
Do you often worry about what others are thinking about you?	☐	☐
Do you forgo your own needs to make sure that everyone else is okay? (E.g., if no one else volunteers for a task, do you end up taking it?)	☐	☐

How many questions did you answer with "yes"? How many with "no"? If you answered four or more questions with "yes," then you may be engaging in codependent behaviors at work.

Now, reflect on the following questions regarding your organization and leader, again checking "yes" or "no" for each.

The Organizations' & Leaders' Behaviors	YES	NO
Does the organization feel chaotic? For example, does it have a lot of emergencies where you're expected to drop everything (even your personal needs)?	☐	☐
Does your boss share personal information (that doesn't belong in the workplace) with the aim of inciting your empathy and caretaking?	☐	☐
Do you overfunction? In other words, are you expected to do work not in your job description for which you're not offered additional compensation or benefits?	☐	☐
Does being self-sacrificial often get rewarded and/or praised?	☐	☐
Is the act of leaving the organization for another company considered a betrayal and/or punished in some way (e.g., if people are cut off or derided)?	☐	☐
Are boundaries not respected? Or resisted in aggressive or passive-aggressive ways?	☐	☐
Does the organization describe itself as a "family" in order to promote a lack of boundaries?	☐	☐

How many questions did you answer with "yes"? How many with "no"? If you answered four or more questions with "yes," then you may be dealing with a codependent organization.

EXERCISE 1.3: REFLECTING ON YOU IN YOUR WORKPLACE

Based on your replies to the previous exercise, are you engaging in codependent behavior at work? If so, which behaviors are a struggle for you? Can you identify where they originate from in your own personal history? Do you think you're working in a codependent organization? If so, what are the indicators?

_____

_____

_____

_____

Now, let's take a break from your situation and view the topic through a different lens.

CASE STUDY: SHANICE

Shanice was an assistant professor in psychology at the university where she got her bachelor's degree. This was what she always imagined she'd be pursuing—what she trained to do for over a decade. Throughout the first years of her professorship, the research she presented at seminars was minimized by her colleagues. She has felt continually dismissed and marginalized. Her mentor couldn't care less about her tenure process and was very disconnected; he often canceled the one-on-ones she set up with him. Conversely, she herself was overloaded with advisees—since she was one of the few people of color on the faculty, she was regularly sought out by those needing her guidance. She felt alone in her research and had few collaborators. She felt stuck and couldn't imagine another option. She feared she might not be good enough to get tenure, or even become a full professor. Overworked and burned out, she struggled to envision a brighter future.

EXERCISE 1.4: HELPING SHANICE RETHINK HER DREAMS

Part of the experience of impostor syndrome is that we often feel limited in what we can do, and where we can be creative and expansive about our opportunities. So, let's practice this on Shanice's behalf. What are some other possibilities for Shanice? How do we help Shanice think about options outside what she knows? What resources can she use? How can she reimagine her dreams? What does she need to consider? What may be keeping her stuck? How can she work on loosening those tethers?

_____

_____

_____

_____

When you're feeling stuck and without options in a job track, it can be helpful to consider what you value about this career path. What brings you a sense of joy? What creates your commitment to this job path? Perhaps a skill set you enjoy using? Or a particular outcome you seek? (For example, Shanice values that she gets to produce research that contributes to her field.)

Consider: is this the *only* place where you can use this skill set or produce this outcome? Are there other options? If you can't think of any, who else that you already know might have some ideas? What relationships could you build to expose you to other options?

We use the example of Shanice as an academic because often in academic paths it is thought that there is only one option: being a professor—ideally a tenured professor. But even in a career that isn't as linear as academia, we can feel there are few options for us. But that's not true—even in academia. So it's critical to break this notion as you dismantle your impostor syndrome.

It has been noted that there are more than ten thousand possible career options, and even more opportunities will be created as technology develops further. So we want you to think expansively about your options, because limited and contracted ideas about your future will keep you locked in unhealthy work environments. Even if, in your family when you were a child, you felt locked in a toxic environment, remember that work is not family. You have more autonomy here in the world of work, and you have more options—but only if you see them.

Let's demonstrate this with the example of Shanice. If what she values most about her career path is her research, she could consider working at a research institute. She could consider consulting opportunities to parlay her research to a business setting. She could explore opportunities within corporations that have behavioral research centers. She could forge into the entrepreneurial realm and create her own company. She could open her own clinical practice—after getting licensed if necessary—with a training arm dedicated to practically applying the research she specializes in.

The skill of thinking expansively is crucial to combating your impostor syndrome. Commit to thinking that feeling "secure" is no longer why you will stay in a position where you feel trapped. Explore what keeps you trapped. Is it a lack of knowledge about other options? Is it that you can't create financial safety nets for yourself? Is it a false sense of security (e.g., the stability of having any job)? Is it an unnecessary loyalty to a boss or company? Is it familiarity with things that are known?

EXERCISE 1.5: REFLECTING ON WHAT KEEPS YOU STUCK

Consider if any of the questions above spark ideas about why you get stuck in a role. What are your particular vulnerabilities to getting stuck? Can you address them in new ways that help free you? How can you identify them when they occur? Can you make a plan to not get caught in them again?

_____

_____

_____

_____

_____

CODEPENDENCY: DETACHING FROM OTHERS' APPROVAL

As we shared in *Own Your Greatness,* codependent family dynamics are often the foundation of the impostor syndrome mindset. As we focus on our own dream, breaking codependent patterns becomes incredibly important to moving forward. We will discuss codependence several times in this book, and in different contexts. Here, we want to focus specifically on the aspect of codependence that incites people-pleasing and seeking others' approval. For example:

- Seeking external validation of our accomplishments, in part to guide our future goals.
- Prioritizing mentorship relationships for the approval we can get from them.
- Hyperfocusing on negative feedback and prioritizing the areas where you receive this feedback.
- Overvaluing others and undervaluing yourself.
- Not setting boundaries around your time or needs.

Learning to honor your dreams calls for creating detachment from the need for approval. To do that, let's revisit how this gets started in our early childhood experiences. In families that exhibit codependence, the family is often centered around the well-being of a physically or mentally ill person. For example, if your father was an alcoholic, perhaps much of your childhood was centered on staying out of his way when he was drunk and "being a good kid" when he was sober—maybe in the hopes of encouraging his sobriety. So, you often hyperfocused on pleasing others, which became how you felt valuable, valid, or seen in your family. This scenario is one of codependency: where you depend on others for validation, direction, and a sense of stability, and they depend on you for a set of similar reasons. This people-pleasing tendency would naturally continue into adulthood, where you would enact it in any scenario in which you felt responsible to a community.

In this sort of experience, your own needs would be minimized because they paled in comparison to the needs of that central family member. As a result, you'd learned to suppress your needs and not protest when others ignored them. But now, while we work on moving beyond codependency and the impostor syndrome that comes from it, we need to learn how to emphasize your needs, your goals, and your own, *internal* assessment of your performance rather than always looking outward to see what others think, what others need, and if there is room for you.

In a healthy family system, there is room for everyone to have their needs met, regardless of their situation. It doesn't have to be "either-or"—it can be "both-and." We're going to help you not suppress what you need just because (you sense) someone else has larger needs. You have the right to your needs and your goals. In the exercise to follow, consider the dynamics that left your needs unmet.

EXERCISE 1.6: FAMILY TRIGGERS FOR DENYING YOUR NEEDS

What are the dynamics in your family that caused you to silence your needs?

_____

_____

_____

What messages did you receive that enforced that you had to be pleasing to be seen?

_____

_____

_____

As a result, what makes it hard to set emotional boundaries around others' approval?

_____

_____

_____

How is it showing up in your current work life or in respect to your dreams?

_____

_____

_____

Part of the process of letting go of approval-seeking comes from understanding where it comes from and what it serves—and then thinking about ways to fulfill your needs in healthier manners.

CASE STUDY: ANASTASIA

Anastasia was a forty-three-year-old attorney. She'd achieved some impressive milestones in her career—including being promoted to general counsel for her company. However, she never felt good enough for her position—she just felt she knew how to be in the right place at the right time. Her spouse was very supportive, but the compliments and support were never enough to boost her up. She had a very difficult relationship with her mother. She always sought her mother's approval, and wanted her mother to understand what she did in her work and to be proud of her, but her mother never showed any interest.

Part of Anastasia's struggle was her inability to internalize her own accomplishments without the acknowledgment of her mother. This dynamic is part of what prevented her from ever feeling "good enough." This is a very common dynamic with codependence, where we constantly seek approval from people who aren't inclined to give it—which can just make us want it all the more.

Anastasia's task was to accept her mother and her limitations, mourn the loss of the mother she needed and wanted, and work to mother herself—to give herself the support, approval, care, and visibility she needed. Clearly, this is easier said than done. Since some of this kind of work is difficult (and lonely) to do alone, it can greatly help to reach out to others for support. (See Build a Dream Team below.)

BUILD A DREAM TEAM

In Chapter 9 of *Own Your Greatness* we recommend creating a "Dream Team" of supporters to offer guidance throughout your journey of working on your dreams. To follow are ideal candidates for your team:

- **Mentor:** A mentor is someone who is senior to you in their accomplishments and successful in at least some aspects of their career. It's actually ideal to have more than one, since different experts can offer varied perspectives and contacts. Look for mentors who are good at providing constructive feedback, offering relationship connections, and helping you identify new opportunities.
- **Cheerleader:** The cheerleader helps you highlight and celebrate wins and accomplishments. This person is often full of emotional support and positivity.
- **Grounder:** The grounder helps you put things into perspective. Let's say you made a mistake or feel you're in some sort of crisis; the grounder helps you regain your footing by reframing the situation in a way that makes it feel recoverable.
- **Action Planner:** The action planner supports you in considering what steps you might take when you're stuck or caught in the impostor syndrome cycle.
- **The Big-Picture Person:** It's really easy to hyperfocus on the present, which can distract us from pursuing our ultimate goals. The big-picture person helps you to take a long view at what might be possible in the future.
- Additional roles include a therapist and a career coach.

For more, see Chapter 9 of *Own Your Greatness.*

Now, before we turn to the next two exercises, let's consider some of the different ways this experience shows up for you. Do you need others to always approve of you? Do you struggle with disapproval? If others doubt you or think you can't do something, do you try to prove them wrong? Are you able to appreciate your own accomplishments? Or do you need someone else to approve of them first?

EXERCISE 1.7: REFLECTING ON YOUR CODEPENDENCE

What do you need to work on in order to let go of seeking approval from others? What's your plan to proceed with that work? (For example, will you work on that with a therapist? Will you use tools you already have but haven't been using?)

_____

_____

_____

_____

_____

EXERCISE 1.8: WHAT'S YOUR APPROVAL PICTURE?

First, draw a picture that reflects how your people-pleasing and approval-seeking look to you. Can you visualize a healthier way you could please others and receive the approval you seek? Draw how that could look. Feel free to include whatever words describe the two images.

TAKING CARE OF YOUR INNER CHILD

Your inner child represents the younger version of yourself that exists within you and carries the difficult moments that you were unable to process because you didn't have the skills or abilities to do so at the time. Your inner child can carry the hurt, pain, sadness and also hopes, dreams, and possibilities.

Let's talk about a technique for moving away from seeking others' approval. When we were children and developing our sense of self, we needed parents, teachers, and caregivers to reflect back to us how we were doing to help us to develop a sense of who we are. Since it's likely that these parents, teachers, and caregivers didn't always get what they needed, they sometimes didn't give us exactly what we needed—or they didn't give it in a way that was useful to us. Continually seeking this validation from them will *not* help us heal from this and move in a different direction. What *will* help us has three stages. We need to take the time to consider what we need and look for from others. We need to work on forgiving ourselves and them for this unhelpful process we've been engaging in. And we need to reflect on how we can give ourselves what we need.

EXERCISE 1.9: TAKING CARE OF YOURSELF

What did you need that you didn't get from parents, caregivers, and teachers? What did you need to hear? What were you looking for?

_____

_____

_____

Have you forgiven the caretakers who didn't fulfill (all) your needs? Have you forgiven yourself for having those needs? If not, what's getting in the way?

_____

_____

_____

How do you start giving *yourself* what you need? How can you get better at receiving from yourself?

_____

_____

_____

A NOTE ON FORGIVENESS

It's important to remember that forgiveness is not for the other person—forgiveness is for you. Forgiveness does not mean approving of what they did, deciding it was "okay." Forgiveness means bearing witness for yourself regarding what happened and letting go of the unfinished dynamic between you. It's unhealthy to keep hoping for something that may never come, such as your pain being acknowledged by the person who hurt you, or wanting some insight on their part that changes their behavior. But you can give to yourself. You can bear witness. You can honor your experience. You can set boundaries. And you can accept the past and let it go. You can forgive yourself. Forgiving yourself can be a significant part of forgiving others because we sometimes hold ourselves responsible for aspects of the experience.

Learning how to give ourselves what we need, how to care for ourselves and our dreams, is akin to parenting ourselves—or reparenting ourselves. You may not have gotten what you needed or wanted when you were young, but you are capable of giving it to yourself in exactly the way that would be best for you. Approaching your hurts in this way can give you such a powerful relationship with yourself and can help you know yourself in completely new ways. Reparenting yourself can be crucial to breaking the habit of seeking external validation. But note: the point is not that you can never enjoy external validation; that form of validation can help you internalize your strengths and accomplishments. The point is to not rely on external validation as your sole form of validation, and to not seek validation from unhealthy or triggering people. Ideally, you can also cultivate validating yourself.

EXERCISE 1.10: VISUALIZING YOUR INNER CHILD

Close your eyes and think about your inner child. Allow yourself to see the younger you. The you that seeks validation. The you that wants others to like you so badly. Picture this younger you in detail. Once you have a clear picture, ask yourself these questions:

How old are you? _____

What do you feel about yourself?

_____

_____

What are you looking for?

_____

_____

Why are you looking for these things?

_____

_____

What do you need from you?

_____

_____

_____

_____

Is there a nickname or adjective that might capture you at this time?

_____

Ask yourself, "How can I be better to you?"

_____

_____

_____

Some find this activity difficult, especially if it's hard to get a clear picture of your younger self. So we want you to take the time to get the clearest picture you can and then (again) answer those questions. We want you to really learn to connect with your inner child, and to support that child in meeting their needs. Help to fill what they were missing.

WHY YOUR DREAMS ARE IMPORTANT

This idea of connecting with your inner child is central to reconnecting with the parts of yourself that need to relearn how to dream. If you've struggled with impostor syndrome, you've likely had trouble differentiating *your* dreams from the dreams others have had for you. Allow yourself to find a connection to dreaming expansively. Know that there are a vast number of possibilities for you, and you have the right to explore and find them.

In this process we want you to get into a habit of dreaming about your future and what you want for yourself. And if that feels like a tall order, then we ask that you allow yourself to find the time to practice in consistent, small increments letting go and envisioning the possibilities to dream about your future and what you want for yourself. When you let go of your impostor syndrome, you start to truly realize the depth of possibilities for yourself, and we want you to fully embrace that. We want you to also do this in a newfound way that allows for revising dreams as they morph into something different. This isn't about being rigid about dreams and setting ourselves up for perfectionistic disappointment. This isn't about solely ticking boxes. This is about allowing ourselves to create a path for ourselves that is in tune to who we are and who we are becoming.

EXERCISE 1.11: DREAM-VISIONING PLAN

I plan to take time every (e.g., Saturday, once a month)_____ to work on my dreams, assess my progress toward them, and make any needed changes.

In order to not be perfectionistic about this process, I plan to:

_____

_____

_____

I will visualize my dreams by displaying my dream plans in this way:

_____

_____

Currently, my dreams include:

_____

_____

_____

KEY TAKEAWAYS

In closing this first chapter, we hope that:

- You're aware of what breaking the impostor syndrome cycle means for you.
- You understand how organizational loyalty and codependence work together, and how they may be keeping you trapped in certain situations.
- You see the importance of autonomy in your process of recovering from impostor syndrome.
- You're aware of how "limited" thinking can prevent you from fully grasping the breadth of your dreams.
- You've explored how family codependency dynamics may be contributing to seeking others' approval, and you have some ideas about how to break this up.
- You've done some inner child work to begin to connect with the parts of yourself that seek external validation, and you're learning how to give that to yourself.

Chapter 2

PROTECTING THE DREAM

When you overcome impostor syndrome, you're able to set firmer boundaries, which means refusing to overwork. You're able to fully own your skills and accomplishments. The new you emerges, one who commits to self-care and to a better balance of work and personal life. However, when you do all this, your coworkers may not be as open to this new you. Your work system—which may include your boss, peers, direct reports, and clients—may want you to revert to your old habits of overwork, perfectionism, and loose(r) boundaries. This chapter will explore how to introduce to the world the new you—one who is no longer ruled by impostor syndrome—in order to sustain your healthier work habits. This chapter will also discuss how to respond when your work environment is not receptive to the new you, including how to push back when your work system says "no" to setting better boundaries. We'll cover the importance of refusing to stay stuck in a toxic system so as to sustain a healthier you—as well as how to intentionally celebrate the new you.

INTRODUCING THE NEW YOU: INCREASING AGENCY

Once you conquer impostor syndrome, it can feel like the world has opened to you—even that you've become a brand-new person. You can feel a new sense of agency, the capacity to have the power and resources to fulfill your potential and impact your life. The new you, however, needs to be introduced to your current work environment, which may be a bit of a challenge. Since the system is so used to the old you—who showed up in spaces significantly influenced by impostor syndrome—it may take some time for them to adjust and accept the new you.

However, that shouldn't deter you from introducing and protecting the new you. So, in introducing the new you, you want to emphasize the following points:

- You have stronger boundaries and will no longer overwork so as to please others or to prove you belong.
- You own your value and competence, and will no longer shrink yourself to make others comfortable.
- You prioritize your self-care and will take more vacation and PTO (personal time off).
- You no longer regard burnout as a badge of honor.
- You do not see perfection as the goal, but rather as a barrier to growth and learning.

The following case study describes just one way of how this scenario could play out.

CASE STUDY: GINNY

Ginny was the senior associate director of advisement at a large public college. Ginny had three direct reports, two peers, and her boss, who was the director of advisement. For the eight years she'd been employed at the office of advisement, Ginny steadily worked her way up the ranks, starting as a graduate student intern. Because of the way she grew into the role, she always believed that to keep her position she had to consistently prove her competence. She regularly compared herself to new hires, who had more prestigious degrees and a lot more experience than she had—which left her always feeling lacking. So she overcompensated for that perceived "lack." She stayed extra hours to see more students during registration time. She regularly volunteered to represent the office at events, even on Saturdays. She took calls outside of her work time. She never said "no." As a result, she constantly felt burned out. She often got very sick at the end of the academic year and spent a significant part of her summer recovering.

But Ginny decided she wanted a different life and realized that her impostor syndrome was keeping her stuck in a steady state of fear. After working through Own Your Greatness, *she was able to really improve her impostor syndrome. She realized she no longer had to overwork or prove that she was worthy of her role. She was so excited to finally approach her job differently.*

By recognizing the costs of impostor syndrome, Ginny developed into a new person. But she understood that she would face resistance at work. For one thing, the office culture rewarded overwork, and since her role was the "go-to" person to fix issues, she was expected to constantly be in work mode. Ginny knew that her boss and colleagues would be unhappy about her new self showing up at work. She felt nervous about making some hard decisions that would not be received well. However, she maintained her boundaries and protected her new self. And although her colleagues and boss were initially taken aback, they soon acclimated to the change and responded positively.

EXERCISE 2.1: INTRODUCING THE NEW YOU

Describe how you would like to introduce the new you to your workplace. What words or characteristics would you use to emphasize your new approach to work after defeating impostor syndrome? (For example, "more focused on my self-care," "invested in setting better boundaries," etc.)

_____

_____

_____

_____

CULTIVATING AUTONOMY

As we work on creating a healthy relationship with both our work environments and ourselves in these environments, maintaining respect for our autonomy can demonstrate to others how we wish for them to respect and value us. When we value ourselves, we're less likely to stand for behaviors intended to diminish us. Note that focusing on your value and autonomy is not about being against collaboration, community, or teamwork. On the contrary—it can make you a better collaborator; in respecting yourself, you know how important it is to respect others and their autonomy. Even if you previously hid your impostor syndrome by being a "lone wolf," you now know how important community is to overcoming impostor syndrome. We want to make sure that we do not reinforce any behaviors related to impostor syndrome—in relation to ourselves or to others.

EXERCISE 2.2: PRACTICING AUTONOMY

In answering the questions that follow, consider how you can work on practicing autonomy in your everyday work life.

SKILL	REFLECTION QUESTIONS	RESPONSES
Boundaries	How can you set better boundaries? What would these boundaries look like? How will you hold yourself accountable when you get pushback?	
Self-Evaluation	What are your own markers for success? How do you know you are doing well? How can you notice areas for development without being harsh with yourself?	
Tolerance for Conflict and Disagreement	How can you work on managing disagreement without overfocusing on pleasing others? What do you fear about expressing disagreement with others? Where is the evidence that those fears will come true if you express a contrary opinion?	
Prioritization of Self-Care	How is your self-care structured into your routine? How do you ensure that your self-care is part of your work process? How do you make sure it's nonnegotiable?	
Valuing Yourself	How do you work on making sure your needs are being honored? How do you appreciate yourself? What do you contribute to a situation without needing external validation?	

• • •

EXPANDING YOUR DREAMS

Another significant aspect of crafting your dreams is having a breadth and depth of understanding about the professional possibilities out there. People-pleasers often pursue career interests that make other people proud or that we excel at even if it's not our passion. We can be limited to our established environment. We can often be fearful of taking a risk by looking outside the small circle of what we know. But as we continue our work combating impostor syndrome and building on our dreams, we have to push out of that circle. We need to focus on being exposed to new things, pushing our competencies further outside our comfort zone, and considering how to use our talents and skills in ways that create flexibility and increase our options.

SETTING STRONG BOUNDARIES

When you overcome impostor syndrome and recognize you don't need to overwork or take on roles that sustain impostor syndrome (like Superperson, Knowledge Hub, Behind-the-Scenes Leader), you're able to instead focus on yourself while honoring your talents. But in doing so you'll need to set new, stronger boundaries to protect your dreams. Those boundaries may include signing off from work at an earlier time, not responding to emails or texts after work or on weekends, and declining requests that would deplete your self-care time. Introducing others to the new you means letting them know about your new boundaries.

One of the challenges of introducing new boundaries is the concern about the response you'll get. Many of our clients have shared with us the backlash they received when attempting to establish new boundaries—how some simply refused to respect those boundaries. You might be worried that introducing new boundaries would cause a rift in your relationship with friends and colleagues—and therefore refrain from setting those boundaries. But as we move through our impostor syndrome we know we need to grow beyond people-pleasing and conflict avoidance. We have to work on these habits and behaviors and try new, more healthy ways of relating to others.

While it is true, unfortunately, that some people won't respond well to these boundaries—either because they want to exploit your overwork to their benefit, or they want you to remain with them in a constant state of work-life imbalance—those who are genuinely concerned about you will definitely support you. Maintaining boundaries is not about being selfish or not caring for others; rather, it's about protecting the new you and the dream you've created to live a healthier and more balanced life. Therefore, it's important to recognize that those who truly care about your well-being will understand and will want to support you as you forge this new way of working. It will also take a period of adjustment for yourself and for others—and so, try to not be dismayed with the initial difficulty in maintaining boundaries, and definitely don't give up. It's part of the process to face resistance. And it's critical that you be patient with yourself and with others, gently reminding them when needed about the new boundaries you have created.

TIPS FOR DEALING WITH RESISTANCE TO CHANGE

- Help others feel they're a part of the change. For example, if your boss has encouraged you to take care of yourself, then relate that you're now setting your boundary in response to their feedback.

- Try to understand the nature of the resistance and see if you can address it; there might be an easy way to address what they're concerned about.

- Implement your changes in small increments. For example, if you previously stopped working at 10:00 p.m. every night, try logging off at 9:00 p.m. for a while, followed by incrementally earlier still.

- Strive to effectively communicate the change. In other words, don't speak angrily or reactively. Just clearly state what will occur/what your boundaries entail, and then calmly address any concerns expressed about your changes.

- Find allies who support you. It's easier to make changes and get support when there are others doing the same—especially if you have strategic support at higher levels of leadership.

CASE STUDY: GINNY (continued from page 31)

Ginny began telling her coworkers she would no longer respond to concerns communicated outside of work hours. She encouraged them to consider their most pressing needs during the week and to schedule time on her calendar if needed. Should any issue come up after their meeting, she suggested they send her a detailed email with their questions and possible needs. Ginny then conveyed she'd try to respond within twenty-four hours, but if it was during the weekend she'd respond on Monday. Initially, Ginny's colleagues and boss had some trouble respecting her boundaries, but slowly—as Ginny maintained them and reminded her team members about them—she was able to sustain a much more balanced work experience.

EXERCISE 2.3: ESTABLISHING NEW BOUNDARIES

Take some time to write down the new boundaries you need to establish at work (e.g., setting a consistent end time, not responding to emails at all hours, etc.). Jot down your fears about establishing those boundaries. On a scale of 1 to 10, how likely are those fears to come true? If they come true, what can you do about them?

_____

_____

_____

_____

PUSHING BACK WHEN THE SYSTEM SAYS "NO"

Ideally, your work system will be accommodating when you introduce this new you, establish appropriate boundaries, and reduce your burnout practices. Unfortunately, the reality is that some systems benefit so much from your impostor syndrome and the old you that they will refuse to accept the new you. When the system says "no," it may feel like you have no power in the process, and that you need to just go along with the dysfunctional nature of your workplace. However, protecting your dream and continuing to own your greatness means recognizing that you do have options and you do have power. You can protect the new you by deciding whether to utilize that power or to explore other options.

CASE STUDY: ANDRE

Andre was a marketing manager for a small advertising agency. As he overcame his impostor syndrome, he was able to reduce his work hours and to establish a much more pleasant life routine. His new practice of having a set start and end time and refusing to overwork left him feeling generally less stressed. Then his company landed a new client—an occurrence that always sent his supervisor into panic mode. His boss was a very anxious person; she tended to overwork herself and the team, even though it wasn't really necessary. So she began to make demands of Andre's time, frequently scheduling meetings outside his scheduled work hours. Unfortunately, her meetings weren't very productive: she often didn't have a clear work plan, she discussed aspects of the project on a piecemeal basis with no coherent vision, and she assigned parts of the project to team members on the fly. Andre knew projects could be approached much more efficiently, but he'd always just obliged and suffered in silence. The same routine started to play itself out again, with his boss scheduling last-minute meetings outside his work hours. Each time he tried to end his day, she would ask him to complete one more task, making it impossible for him to leave. He realized that his current work system was saying "no" to his desire to set appropriate boundaries. He knew he'd need to push back even more assertively to ensure that his impostor syndrome did not return full force, letting him fall back into old, bad habits of overworking and neglecting his self-care.

Andre suspected that his supervisor's anxieties were triggered by the uncertainty of new projects. (In fact, he wondered if she herself suffered from impostor syndrome.) Her way of coping was to constantly discuss the project in meetings even though that wasn't an effective use of their time. So Andre decided to confront the situation directly and set up a one-on-one meeting with his boss. When she anxiously questioned what the meeting would cover, he said he merely wanted to go over some process components. During that meeting, Andre affirmed his desire to effectively contribute to the project's success—and then introduced a comprehensive project plan that clearly outlined the responsibilities of each team member, timelines for each deliverable, planned check-in meetings to discuss progress, and anticipated results. She was very impressed by his plan and said she'd review it further to make some changes—but that it looked good from an initial glance. Subsequently, the team met to discuss the work plan, which was fully adopted. Thankfully, the early morning and late-night meetings ceased, and Andre was able to go back to his well-balanced routine.

If the system says "no" to your attempts to keep your boundaries intact and the new you safe, you'll want to consider what your options are and how to respond. Think about ways you can assert your power to push back. Sometimes, it may seem that the only two options are to acquiesce to the system by giving up your boundaries—or to leave the resistant system by quitting your job. Among the clients we've worked with, some instances did call for separating from the toxic system. Fortunately, as in Andre's case, there are oftentimes other options to explore. Some of our clients were able to change managers or transfer to another area, which helped them to protect their boundaries and their new selves. Others developed allies within their department to collectively demand a new work culture. By evaluating the situation, you may come to realize that you can impact the system by solving a perceived problem, such as a lack of clarity, or worry about a client project. Or you might find it's not a systems problem but rather a bad manager problem. Dissecting how your work environment is saying "no" to the new you and your boundaries can help you determine your options, your power in the process, and how to push back to protect the new you. For more, see the Ways to Reassert One's Boundaries sidebar on the next page.

WAYS TO REASSERT ONE'S BOUNDARIES

- Communicate your experiences in a non-defensive manner that includes how a change could be beneficial to all.
- Study the process components (e.g., meetings that are scheduled at 4:30 p.m. when you end work at 5 p.m.) and consider how to change them systematically.
- Assess the people factors (e.g., a workaholic boss who doesn't like to respect boundaries) and what can be tackled there.
- Build a coalition of others who feel similarly and create a plan together.
- Utilize resources like HR to develop solutions.
- Get senior leadership involved strategically.

EXERCISE 2.4: ADDRESSING PUSHBACK

Write down three ways your current work environment is saying "no" to your attempts to set boundaries, to not overwork, and to decrease your impostor syndrome.

1. _____

2. _____

3. _____

Develop three ways that you can assert your power to establish/maintain appropriate boundaries.

1. _____

2. _____

3. _____

What are your concerns about doing so? What are some ways to address those concerns?

_____

_____

_____

IDENTIFYING A TOXIC SYSTEM

Let's say you've explored all your options and have attempted to respond to pushback when the system says "no"—and yet you're still struggling to protect the new you. It may be that your boss continues to expect responses from you during the weekends and late at night, or your coworkers constantly schedule meetings in your calendar during your break time, even after you've given them feedback about your new boundaries. In situations like that it may be time to leave. Although leaving may not be your preferred option, and it's not one to be taken lightly, it may be the best move to ensure you don't fall back into old habits that are not beneficial to your overall career and personal well-being. It can feel easier to suffer in a system you already know than to risk seeking a new and healthier system. When you're in a toxic system, you may come to believe that all work systems are toxic. That is not the case. What's important is being honest with yourself in considering if your current environment exceeds an acceptable norm of toxicity. Examine the costs of staying: how do they measure up against the perceived benefits of staying? To follow are some guidelines for considering both costs and benefits.

COSTS OF STAYING IN A TOXIC SYSTEM

There are a variety of costs to staying in toxic system:

Constant triggering of your impostor syndrome: This is a heavy cost—and one of the primary reasons we wrote this book. If you remain in a toxic system you may find it difficult to keep your impostor syndrome at bay.

Physical and mental health issues: It's one thing to think you can handle a continuously difficult work environment, but don't forget the fact that high levels of stress can result in major physical and mental health issues, such as hypertension, chronic headaches, sleep disruption, anxiety, burnout, and depression.

Damage to important relationships: If you need to focus time and energy on dealing with a toxic system, you may become so consumed that you neglect important relationships with your partner, friends, or family members—which can result in isolation or decreased social support, which in turn can lead to the physical and mental issues just mentioned.

Learned helplessness: If you feel unable to remove yourself from a toxic system, it's easy to believe that you're helpless—that you have no agency, and there's nothing you can do but suffer. This mentality is called "learned helplessness," and it is strongly linked to depression, burnout, and other mental health issues.

Hopelessness: This is related to learned helplessness, when each day feels like a heavy grind, and you feel your situation will never improve.

Decreased compensation and lack of career advancement: According to the Bureau of Labor Statistics, the average tenure of a wage and salary worker was 4.1 years in 2020.[2] If you stay too long in a job with no growth prospects, your lifetime earnings can decrease by as much as 50 percent.[3] Therefore, staying in a toxic system can stifle your career at a great financial cost.

Imbalance in loyalty: You may feel inclined to stay because you feel loyal to the organization—and would feel guilty if you left. But what if the organization doesn't reciprocate this loyalty? If you never get a raise, if others are constantly promoted over you, if there are no professional development opportunities for you, then you have an imbalance in loyalty.

General unhappiness about your life: Work consumes so many of our waking hours. If that work is not going well, it will negatively impact your general view of life, which can seep out to taint other parts of your life as well.

PERCEIVED BENEFITS OF STAYING IN A TOXIC SYSTEM

Even if you're aware of the costs of staying in a toxic system, the decision to leave can be hampered if you're convinced of the perceived benefits of staying—such as the following:

Familiarity with the company and role: Change is extremely difficult; for some individuals, the safety of working in familiarity trumps the opportunity to work in a healthier system.

Economic security: For many, the fear of not being able to provide for themselves or their families keeps them stuck in a toxic system—especially if they're well compensated and believe their job security will mean they'll never have to worry about financial issues.

Current flexibility: In the age of remote and hybrid work, some people identify work flexibility as an important reason to remain in a toxic system if that system allows them to negotiate their schedule as they wish—and if they believe a new, healthier position wouldn't have that flexibility.

Insurance and benefits: Job lock due to insurance concerns has been a genuine, long-standing barrier to those who wish to leave a toxic environment. The belief that you will never get such good coverage or other benefits may cause you to endure an unhealthy situation if you don't believe you can find such benefits in a healthier system.

Stability: Belief in the stability of a position is one of the primary reasons some of our clients give for staying in a toxic system, since they'd rather never have to think about navigating the anxiety of a job search and dealing with a rapidly changing job market.

Let's now explore the challenges of navigating the decision to stay in or leave a toxic work situation through the following case study.

CASE STUDY: EVELYN

Evelyn was employee number nine in a tech start-up, where she had worked for six years in product management. She was used to working grueling hours, sometimes ninety-hour weeks—including usually being on call on the weekends, especially during a new product launch. Her CEO tended to micromanage and was constantly unhappy about the team's performance, even though the team consistently met its target goals and his unrealistic expectations. During her time at the company, Evelyn witnessed massive and consistent turnover, especially in the C-suite. The CEO's erratic and toxic behavior led the company to go through three CTOs and two CFOs in just three years. With the recent departure of her direct manager, Evelyn was offered a promotion to fill his role overseeing the whole product management team. She hesitantly accepted but recognized that she would now be reporting directly to the CEO.

Evelyn's introduction to the CEO's micromanagement and toxic leadership style started early in her tenure, but she had always been generally protected by her boss. Now the CEO was prone to rapid-fire texting, which could start after midnight. He demanded phone calls at all hours. Whenever he didn't get what he wanted, he exercised his authority with phrases like, "I pay you to have answers for me now! I'm still trying to figure out if you're the right person for this job!" Evelyn felt choked by anxiety by just the thought of interacting with him. She noticed that on Sundays she felt nauseated and experienced intense headaches.

These health signs were a wake-up call for Evelyn. She was determined to not make the same mistakes she'd made in other jobs, where she stayed too long and ended up burned out and suffering numerous health issues. So, not long into her new position, she reached out to her therapist and began a self-care plan, including taking two mental health days off. She also discussed her options with her mentor. During her time off and following a productive conversation with her mentor, who was very supportive, Evelyn began to consider the pros and cons of staying in such a toxic environment. She came to realize that, no matter how well the company did, the position was not worth her suffering and her poor mental and physical health. Although some colleagues and a few of her friends and family members tried to persuade her that she should stay, Evelyn reached out to a career coach to create a job search plan. Within six months, Evelyn had secured a new role in a better-funded start-up, with more equity, a supportive boss, and a clear career pathway.

EXERCISE 2.5: COSTS/BENEFITS OF BEING IN A TOXIC SYSTEM

If you are currently or have been in a toxic work environment, what are/were the costs of staying? What do/did you see as the perceived benefits? Write down three reasons to stay and three reasons to leave.

_____

_____

_____

_____

SHOULD YOU STAY OR SHOULD YOU GO?

Determining if and when to leave a toxic system is a personal choice for everyone, of course. But if you determine that the costs of staying exceed the benefits, you can conclude it's time to part ways. Fortunately, many have come to recognize, especially after overcoming their impostor syndrome, that no amount of benefits can justify staying in a toxic system.

IDENTIFYING TOXIC POSITIVITY

As we've discussed, our society constantly extols the virtues of stability, perceived economic security, and other benefits of just being employed in a job. So, as Evelyn experienced in her consideration period, you may be inundated with advice to the effect of, "You should feel lucky to even have a job. It's stable and you've got good benefits; what more do you want? No job is perfect." Such statements, usually from family, friends, and colleagues, though supposedly said to be helpful, are a clear example of what we call "toxic positivity." Toxic positivity is a belief that, no matter how difficult or dire a situation is, you should always maintain a positive attitude. While such a mindset would appear to be healthy, what makes it toxic is that this mindset rejects any negative emotions, even when they are called for, in favor of excessive and oftentimes inauthentic positivity. Toxic positivity does not allow for you to express the normal range of human emotions about what you're experiencing, forcing you to "just look on the bright side"—no matter the cost.

TOXIC POSITIVITY PHRASES

Toxic positivity is the belief that, no matter how difficult, depressing, or painful a situation may be, you should always respond with a positive frame of mind. Some toxic positivity phrases include:

- "Good vibes only."
- "You'll get over it."
- "Quitting is not an option."
- "It could be worse."
- "Remember how blessed/fortunate/lucky you are."
- "Think positive thoughts!"

When someone tries to spread toxic positivity, try these responses:

- Ground yourself and pause.
- Share how the statement makes you feel (e.g., invalidated, dismissed, etc.).
- Share what you'd prefer to hear instead.

EXERCISE 2.6: YOUR EXPERIENCE OF TOXIC POSITIVITY

What are some of the toxic positive statements that others have said to you? Are there any that you've said to yourself?

_____

_____

_____

_____

HOW TOXIC SYSTEMS AFFECT YOUR AGENCY

As we explored earlier, a toxic system can deprive you of your agency, which is your ability to use your power and resources to change your life. A toxic system can cause you to feel helpless to impact your current situation, resulting in the following:

Decreased confidence in your ability to manage a job search: Even if you've searched for jobs many times before, a toxic environment can make you feel that you're not equipped to facilitate a job search.

Skepticism about finding healthier organizations: Working in a toxic environment can make you start to believe that *all* organizations are toxic, so why bother leaving your familiar one?

Belief that you have no power: Learned helplessness can prevail, causing you to believe that you have no power to effect transformative change in your life.

SUSTAINING AGENCY IN A TOXIC SYSTEM

When you're in a toxic system, especially when that system impacts your health and your prospects, it's important to have methods for embracing your agency. Here are some tips for retaining your agency:

- Consider and focus on all the areas in which you have power and control (e.g., conducting a job search, speaking to human resources, building alliances/coalitions, increasing your self-care, etc.).
- Document all problematic behavior, including dates, circumstances, people present, statements made, etc.
- Consult with an employment attorney if you feel you're being impacted in particularly negative ways (e.g., you're being scapegoated, you're losing promotion opportunities, your performance is being evaluated negatively for no reason, etc.).
- Reach out to your Dream Team for support and guidance, especially mentors, therapists, and coaches.
- Share what you're going through with supportive friends and family members so you don't feel alone.

EMPLOYMENT ATTORNEY OPTIONS

If you're being treated in a manner that requires professional support in understanding your legal rights and recourse, an employment attorney can be essential. Such an attorney can let you know if there is anything legally actionable about your situation. The attorney can also advise on how to go about certain processes within the organization to make sure that you preserve your rights and protect yourself.

Now, finding an employment attorney can feel daunting, and maybe even too expensive, but here are ways to go about it to find a fit that makes sense for you:

- Consult friends and family, especially those with senior-level roles. (They may know employment attorneys from their networks.)
- Reach out to local and national bar associations.
- Explore local law schools and their legal clinics, since those often include employment law clinics.
- Research legal aid clinics.

EXERCISE 2.7: HOW TOXIC SYSTEMS AFFECT YOUR AGENCY AND YOUR IMPOSTOR SYNDROME

Describe how your current work environment affects your agency and how it impacts your impostor syndrome. What power do you have in dealing with the toxic system?

_____

_____

_____

_____

_____

_____

INTENTIONALLY CELEBRATING YOU— ENJOYING YOUR JOY

In ideal work environments, team successes are celebrated. If you're in a system that doesn't bother to celebrate accomplishments, it's important to identify strategies for you to do so on your own. It's all too easy to dismiss or to minimize successes in favor of focusing on the next goal. However, sustaining your agency in a toxic system calls for honoring your efforts and appreciating your talents. Commit time to intentionally celebrating your achievements. Announce them to those close to you and find rituals that allow you to commemorate them accordingly. Amplify your successes by posting them on your social media channels. While such actions may feel out of character for you—especially posting on social media—it is essential for you to embrace the fact that it is not boastful to celebrate achievements for which you worked hard. Making them public further honors your efforts while enabling you to internalize them so that you can fully own them. Don't let impostor syndrome convince you it was just luck. Allow the new you and your dreams to be appropriately praised and protected.

Enjoying your joy means taking time to have a good time. Increasing your experience of pleasant events will elevate your happiness.

So, what does enjoying your joy look like in practical terms? Here are some examples:

- After an important project is completed, book a vacation to relax and recharge.
- If you met a target goal (hit a sales target, finished a paper, etc.), tell your loved ones, and celebrate over a nice dinner.
- If you receive a promotion or a get a new job, post it on social media.
- If you put in a good effort but the results were not what you wanted, take time to practice kindness with yourself, such as getting a massage or pedicure.
- Take the time to acknowledge and celebrate milestones like birthdays and anniversaries.
- Allow others to celebrate you! Let them take you out to dinner or plan a party in your honor.
- Similarly, take in and appreciate compliments rather than dismissing them.
- Maintain a gratitude journal: record the things for which you're grateful. The more positive things you report, the more positive things you'll remember—and the more joy you'll enjoy.

EXERCISE 2.8: STRATEGIES TO INTENTIONALLY CELEBRATE YOU

Describe strategies for intentionally celebrating yourself. If you find honoring yourself difficult, consider what makes it difficult. How can you overcome this difficulty?

_____

_____

_____

_____

_____

_____

KEY TAKEAWAYS

In closing this chapter, we hope that:

- You understand how to introduce the new you to your work system.
- You explored how to maintain boundaries when the system refuses to respect them.
- You identified the costs/benefits of staying in a toxic system—and how to determine when it's time to leave.
- You learned the impact of toxic systems on your agency—and how to increase your agency within them.
- You developed strategies to intentionally celebrate yourself and to protect your dreams.

Chapter 3

CONQUERING BURNOUT AND PERFECTIONISM

Now that we've reviewed how to introduce the new you to the world and to protect your dream, in Chapter 3 we'll examine two realities of the work world that may also impact your ability to protect your dream: burnout and perfectionism. Later in the chapter we'll discuss the different types of perfectionism, consider the costs and perceived benefits of perfectionism, and then explore how to give it up. But first, we're going to talk about burnout.

BREAKING FREE OF BURNOUT

Burnout tends to be strongly linked to impostor syndrome, since overworking is a typical behavioral response for those struggling with it. Even after you've defeated your impostor syndrome, as you build your dream it's important to consciously reduce practices that can lead to burnout so you can protect the new you.

Since the beginning of the COVID-19 pandemic, burnout has increased, and it continues to be a major factor in many work environments. In 2021, a Gallup poll found that 74 percent of employees reported experiencing burnout, up from 67 percent in 2018.[4] Further, another Gallup study found that there are gender gaps in burnout, with 34 percent of women stating they experience burnout "always" or "very often," compared to 26 percent of men. In addition, women who work in hybrid work situations were at greater risk for burnout (38 percent) than women who worked exclusively remotely (31 percent) or in office settings (34 percent).[5] For far too long, burnout has been viewed as an individual issue, not an organizational one, and many solutions were therefore targeted to the individual. While it is true that individuals can utilize key strategies to prevent or reduce burnout, ultimately it is the organization that needs to facilitate long-term change if we are to drastically reduce burnout. Chapter 3 will explore key causes of burnout, myths about burnout, and strategies one can implement to decrease burnout individually. In a later chapter we will also discuss what healthy leaders can do to reduce burnout from an organizational perspective.

REDUCING CHRONIC BURNOUT

As we discussed in *Own Your Greatness*, when you experience impostor syndrome you may be more prone to meet the needs of the organization and its leaders instead of your own, resulting in chronic experiences of burnout. In particular, characteristics such as perfectionism, the tendency to overwork, and the desire to please others may make you more susceptible to burnout. Let's look at how this played out for our client Joanne.

CASE STUDY: JOANNE

Joanne was a fifth-year associate at a corporate law firm on the partner track. She had consistently been recognized as a star performer and felt very proud of her work at the firm. Early in her time there she had struggled with impostor syndrome—she had constantly overworked and had been very perfectionistic to prove that she belonged at her firm. She came to our practice after taking a medical leave due to the high degree of stress she felt dealing with her job. After identifying her impostor syndrome, Joanne was able to set better boundaries at work, manage expectations regarding her case work, reduce her perfectionism and overwork, and have a healthier style of living. Yet, despite these gains, Joanne still regularly reported feelings of burnout. She would have a few weeks of relief after taking a vacation, but as soon as she started back to work, after a week or so, she would start to feel burnout creep back.

In 2019, the World Health Organization (WHO) classified burnout as an occupational phenomenon and defined it as "a syndrome conceptualized as resulting from chronic workplace stress that has not been successfully managed. Burnout refers specifically to phenomena in the occupational context and should not be applied to describe experiences in other areas of life."[6] While we agree with this assessment in terms of burnout being influenced by your occupation, it is important to note that we don't agree with its notion that burnout is only limited to work. We believe that burnout can be exacerbated by more than work. You can also experience burnout from caregiving, relationships, volunteer and extracurricular activities, and other aspects of your life. So, when you consider your burnout we want you to view it more expansively. Oftentimes when people discuss feelings of burnout they solely discuss feelings of exhaustion. Although fatigue is part of it, burnout includes other dimensions as well.

According to the Eleventh Revision of the International Classification of Diseases (ICD-11), which is published by the WHO, burnout is an occupational phenomenon characterized by three dimensions: feelings of energy depletion or exhaustion, increased mental distance from one's job, or feelings of negativism or cynicism related to one's job; and reduced professional efficacy.[7] Additional symptoms of burnout include dreading work, an inability to separate yourself from work, withdrawing, disengaging, irritability, difficulty sleeping, apathy, anxiety, depression, and hopelessness.

In Joanne's case, all three dimensions and many symptoms were present. Although she was able to get on average six and a half hours of sleep, she constantly felt fatigued, both physically and emotionally. She also would get the Sunday blues: beginning on Sunday afternoons, anticipating the start of her work week filled her with a sense of dread. While the cases she worked on were interesting enough, she did not feel motivated or excited about the work. As a result, she also did not believe she was as effective as she could be.

Let's now consider your experience.

EXERCISE 3.1: SIGNS AND SYMPTOMS OF BURNOUT

Take a look at the signs and symptoms of chronic burnout in the table below. Then consider which you experience in your current position, and how often you've experienced them over the last year (e.g., quarterly, monthly, daily, etc.).

SIGN/SYMPTOM	DO YOU EXPERIENCE IT?	HOW OFTEN?
Depletion/exhaustion		
Mental distancing/cynicism about work		
Reduced efficacy		
Inability to separate yourself from work		

SIGN/SYMPTOM	DO YOU EXPERIENCE IT?	HOW OFTEN?
Irritability		
Difficulty sleeping		
Anxiety		
Depression		
Hopelessness		

• • •

MYTHS ABOUT BURNOUT

Unfortunately, despite constant popular media discussions about burnout, there are still some persistent myths that make it difficult for individuals to address their burnout. Some of the most prevalent are:

Myth 1: *Once you experience burnout, you will never experience it again.* The reality is that once you experience burnout you're actually more susceptible to experiencing it again. Therefore, it's important to understand the causes of your burnout so you can focus on recovery by addressing those causes—and then increasing your self-care to prevent it from happening again.

Myth 2: *It will go away after a nice long vacation.* Although a vacation is helpful, as we have previously discussed, burnout is more than just being extremely tired and needing a break. You should definitely take time off, but during that break it would be good to consider how you're going to intervene or work on particular issues that are responsible for the burnout. Once you return to work, it will be critical to address those issues, like establishing firm time boundaries, setting clear work expectations, creating a reasonable workload with your manager, and providing a sense of control to prevent chronic burnout.

Myth 3: *Only people who are weak or who don't know how to work hard experience burnout.* This myth is particularly troubling, since it attempts to shame people who experience burnout in a way that prevents them from trying to adequately remedy it. As previously mentioned, a 2021 Gallup study found that 74 percent of employees reported experiencing burnout.[8] Therefore, it's clear that this is not about people being weak or not being able to work hard. Burnout is both an individual and a systemic issue.

Myth 4: *Burnout is an individual not an organizational concern.* Along the same lines as the previous myth, this myth is one of the most damaging because it puts the onus of addressing burnout on the employee, not the organization. While it was useful for the WHO to classify burnout as a phenomenon of concern, their phrasing may have unwittingly reinforced the notion that burnout is only an individual problem. However, the reality is that many of the root causes of burnout (e.g., unclear work expectations, lack of control, dysfunctional work dynamics, etc.) are the result of poor managerial and organizational structures—which are all created by the system, yet only experienced by the individual. We need to acknowledge the causes of burnout wherever we find them; the more we acknowledge it, the more company leaders have a responsibility to tackle it from an organizational perspective.

Myth 5: *Constant burnout goes hand in hand with success at work.* The reality is that there is no evidence to suggest that the more you experience burnout, the more successful you will be. In fact, since burnout impacts your physical and mental well-being, there is a higher probability that if you're chronically burned out, you'll be unable to achieve many of your target goals.

EXERCISE 3.2: MYTHS ABOUT BURNOUT

What myths about burnout do you tend to believe, either consciously or unconsciously? How can you more intentionally dispel these myths in your daily routine?

_____

_____

_____

_____

_____

IMPACT OF BURNOUT

Another myth about burnout is that it doesn't have significant consequences. But as you can see below, the effects can be very serious:

Physical Consequences

- Burnout can be a predictor of hypercholesterolemia and type 2 diabetes.

- Burnout is associated with hospitalizations due to cardiovascular disease, musculoskeletal pain, gastrointestinal issues, respiratory problems, obesity, headaches, and mortality under forty-five years old.

Mental Health Consequences

- Burnout can be a predictor of insomnia and depressive symptoms.

- Burnout can lead to hospitalization for mental health disorders.

Occupational Consequences

- Burnout can lead to greater job dissatisfaction, greater absenteeism, and presenteeism.

CAUSES OF BURNOUT

It's important to identify the causes of your burnout so you can feel a sense of agency about possible interventions and be strategic about your plans to overcome it. While this list is not exhaustive, hopefully it gives you an opportunity to reflect on what may be impacting your burnout:

Unclear work expectations: When you're unsure about the priorities of your role, you can easily overwork by making *everything* a priority.

Work-life imbalance: When a larger portion of your time is focused on work, and there is little or no leisure or personal time, this can lead to burnout.

Lack of control: If you don't feel a sense of autonomy to determine your work schedule or the nature of your work, that lack of control can cause burnout.

Lack of social support: Another cause is feeling you don't have sufficient social support, either at work or outside of work.

Dysfunctional work dynamics: The following can all contribute to burnout: a toxic boss or coworker, unreasonable time pressures, too large of a workload, being treated unfairly (e.g., fewer preferable assignments, more critical feedback), high levels of conflict among team members, and factionalism—where you are constantly forced to pick sides between different cliques.

High-performer overload: Elaborating on the heavy workload angle: sometimes the star performers are tasked with more work.

Excessive collaboration: Another angle of overwork is excessive collaboration, which can be problematic in two different ways: when the fact that you're in back-to-back meetings all day leaves no time for you to complete your assignments and responsibilities during work hours, and when no decisions can be made without consulting various parties.

Weak time management: Burnout can also result when others don't respect your time—such as when meetings start late and/or run late, or when deadlines are unreasonably tight.

Note that Michael Mankins and Eric Garton have identified the last three items as the primary causes of burnout.[9]

EXERCISE 3.3: CAUSES OF YOUR BURNOUT

What are the primary causes of your burnout?

1. _____

2. _____

Name three ways they show up in your weekly work life.

1. _____

2. _____

3. _____

CASE STUDY: JOANNE (continued from page 49)

After working with us, Joanne realized that her chronic burnout was being caused by unclear work expectations, lack of control, and work-life imbalance. She was working with a senior partner who did a poor job of assigning tasks intentionally and clearly. Therefore, Joanne found herself going into each week unsure about what tasks were truly hers to tackle and, of those, which ones to prioritize. The senior partner was also difficult to reach, often appearing with a last-minute urgent request but not responding adequately to Joanne's questions. As a result, Joanne often felt she spent a good portion of her days seeking greater clarity, and oftentimes would not get it until the end of her workday, causing her to extend it by two to three hours. In order to reduce her chronic burnout, Joanne requested scheduled weekly meetings with the senior partner in order to outline her tasks, priorities, and timelines into a work plan for the week. With these regular meetings she was able to restore her energy and enthusiasm. She was still working hard, but the added clarity enabled her to better balance her life and enjoy her job again.

As in Joanne's case, even an extended vacation or a leave of absence does not make the burnout just go away. In order to deal with the ever-evolving nature of work and continued threats of burnout, we need to be proactive and intentional in addressing its causes—while also increasing self-care to counter the fatigue of its effects. The following extended exercise can help you come up with a new approach to overcome burnout.

EXERCISE 3.4: ADDRESSING CAUSES OF BURNOUT

Consider which of the primary contributors to burnout feel relevant to your experience. Write down your answers to the following questions.

Unclear Work Expectations

1. What are my primary duties for this role?

_____

_____

2. What should be my top three priorities for successfully meeting the expectations of this role?

_____

_____

_____

3. When I'm not clear about shifting expectations, who can provide clarity for me?

_____

_____

Work-Life Imbalance

4. What is driving work-life imbalance? (E.g., impostor syndrome, lack of pleasant activities outside of work, systemic pressure to constantly work, etc.)

_____

_____

5. If I could map out my ideal balanced day, what would it look like?

_____

_____

6. How can I bring my life into greater balance with my work? (E.g., work fewer hours per week, take breaks during the day, schedule regular time off, find hobbies, etc.)

_____

_____

Dysfunctional Work Dynamics

7. What aspects of my workplace are dysfunctional? (E.g., toxic boss/coworker(s), overly competitive work environment, high-conflict culture, etc.)

_____

_____

8. What are some ways I might address these dysfunctional dynamics?

_____

_____

9. If I cannot change these dysfunctional dynamics, what options should I pursue to deal with them? (E.g., confront them directly, seek allies to discuss how to address them, etc.)

_____

_____

Lack of Control

10. What areas of my work life are in my control? What areas are not in my control? (E.g., case assignments, schedule, etc.)

_____

_____

11. What are the areas in which I would like to have greater control?

_____

_____

12. How can I gain greater control over these areas? (E.g., discuss with supervisor or coworkers, etc.)

_____

_____

13. If I cannot gain greater control, how do I handle this lack of control? (E.g., seek support, ask for help, etc.)

_____

_____

Lack of Social Support

14. What type of social support am I seeking? (E.g., guidance from mentors, catching up with friends, engaging socially with colleagues, etc.)

_____

_____

15. What may make it difficult to find the type of social support I want? Am I reluctant to ask for it?

_____

_____

16. How can I intentionally explore how to gain greater social support?

_____

_____

Excessive Collaboration

17. What meetings or collaborations keep me from completing all my tasks during work hours?

_____

_____

18. Oftentimes the agenda of a meeting requires real-time interaction among team members. But some end goals can be reached via "asynchronous" methods such as email or team apps. Could any of these meetings or collaborations be handled in another way?

_____

_____

19. For the times we need to meet in real time, are there any ways to make our time together more productive? (E.g., can we change the cadence of meetings, have a set agenda?)

_____

_____

Weak Time-Management Disciplines

20. In what ways are time-management issues affecting me? (The ways I manage my own time? The ways others disrupt my time-management efforts with interruptions, impromptu meetings, etc.?)

_____

_____

21. What can I do to support better time management for myself and my team members?

_____

_____

Now, having reflected on the various causes of your burnout, name three actions you can take to address them.

1. _____

2. _____

3. _____

We hope that the above exercise can help you regain some sense of control over your work life so you can begin to tackle your burnout head-on. Take a moment now to honor what you're learning and respect what you're hearing from yourself.

IDENTIFYING BURNOUT PRACTICES

In order to address our burnout, we also need to first identify the burnout practices in which we engage. Burnout practices are those behaviors that lead us to overwork, ignore our self-care, and push us to the brink of burnout time and again. Some of us maintain this overwork mentality because we believe it is this type of behavior that made us successful. Even those of us who've conquered our impostor syndrome can still be fearful of letting these burnout practices go—under the false assumption that, without them, we'd be unable to maintain our level of success. Some of these practices include:

• Never taking a break during the workday.

- Constantly checking emails and notifications during the weekends and after work hours—even when there are no pressing issues.
- Never using sick days and never taking a vacation or PTO—as though such dedication to the job were a badge of honor.
- (Demonstratively) working when you're sick—"presenteeism."
- Taking pride in being the person who works the most hours on your team.
- Believing that the only way to show that you're doing a good job is by working yourself to the point of near collapse.

When your impostor syndrome is triggered, it is easy to resort to the burnout practices you know best. Breaking free of burnout means truly letting go of burnout practices.

EXERCISE 3.5: BURNOUT PRACTICES

Describe the types of burnout practices you tend to engage in.

_____

_____

_____

_____

_____

UNCOVERING THE HIDDEN PURPOSE OF BURNOUT PRACTICES

Burnout practices can also serve a specific purpose for you: namely, to keep you distracted from other, more uncomfortable activities, such as dealing with your anxiety, sitting still with your thoughts, or having to confront a difficult relationship. If there is a hidden purpose behind your burnout practices, recognizing that purpose is a first step toward helping you proactively address those other issues—which will increase your overall well-being.

EXERCISE 3.6: HIDDEN REASONS FOR YOUR BURNOUT

Be honest with yourself and take a moment to consider what else your burnout might be serving. Describe some possible hidden purposes of your burnout practices.

_____

_____

_____

_____

_____

Now that you've been honest with yourself, take a moment to reflect on what you might do instead. How might you more directly address the things that your burnout is helping you avoid?

_____

_____

_____

_____

DISCONNECTING FROM AN IDEOLOGY OF BURNOUT

The ideology of burnout encourages you to rate yourself every day in terms of work productivity. Rather than being kind to yourself, paying attention to what you need and want, you instead feel the need to grade yourself each evening. Disconnecting from the ideology of burnout means creating new measures for productivity and viewing your value more expansively. Moving away from the notion that the only way to judge your day is by work output will help to eliminate an ideology of burnout. Instead, being productive can mean spending more time meditating or exercising each day—which in fact can increase your productivity when you're addressing work tasks. Overcoming burnout ideology can mean not evaluating yourself in terms of productivity at all—and instead finding other ways to evaluate your day, such as by how much you enjoyed, how much you learned, how in touch you were with yourself, and how much you felt a sense of connection to the moment. It means seeing your value not only in what you produce, but also with whom you engage, and how you care for yourself and others.

CASE STUDY: LISA (continued from page 11)

Prior to quitting her toxic job, when Lisa's impostor syndrome was triggered, she would immediately focus her efforts on productivity, especially the number of tasks she could complete in a day. She did this because work was an area over which she felt a sense of control and in which she felt valuable. So, she could go into overwork mode. Therefore, when Richard would ask her about her day, if it had gone well in terms of task completion she would say, "It was productive." If it hadn't, she would beat herself up and report, "It was not really productive. I didn't get a lot of things done." Each day was evaluated by the number of work tasks that could be checked off her list—rather than holistically considering additional aspects, such as how much self-care time she'd provided for herself, or even how much she'd enjoyed her day. She was being influenced by the ideology of burnout.

EXERCISE 3.7: BURNOUT IDEOLOGY DEFEATED

Describe how you can change your definition of daily productivity and success (e.g., not rating your efforts every day, viewing self-care as a productive activity, not tying your value to work output, etc.).

_____

_____

_____

_____

_____

GIVING UP PERFECTIONISM

Perfectionism is not a characteristic that you should retain when introducing the new you to the world. There is a strong correlation between perfectionism and impostor syndrome, as you may feel you have no room to make a mistake or you will be exposed as a fraud. Yet even after defeating impostor syndrome, you may find it difficult to give up perfectionism if you consider it critical to your long-term success.

Perfectionism shows up in strange and contradictory ways in impostor syndrome. It can lead to overwork and meticulousness, which requires you to maintain an unrealistic productivity. It can also create self-sabotage: if you fear you won't be able to complete something perfectly, it's easy to procrastinate as an avoidance method of coping with the anxiety—which can set you up for mixed results at best, or failure at worst.

Perfectionism also can be highly connected to people-pleasing. Often, we develop perfectionistic tendencies in childhood if we were only considered worthy when we delivered what others wanted or expected from us. That scenario can lead us to focus on external validation—always demonstrating our value by consistently producing and delivering at the highest level. This is one of the reasons recovering from perfectionism can be so scary. We can feel that not being perfect will lead us to not being loved, not being seen, or not being even considered. And so, as we work to challenge our perfectionism, it's important to look toward relationships that can support and accept us in all states—both when we are achieving and when we are failing. Ideally we can surround ourselves with people who embrace us in the fullness of who we are.

Another reason it can be so challenging to give up perfectionism is because it's often seen in such a positive light. However, such unimpeachable high standards, which are then reinforced by yourself and others, can create internal pain and interpersonal struggle. The result of perfectionism is often deriding yourself for not being enough, criticizing others for not being enough, and being constantly unsatisfied. Perfectionism can often make you feel alone as you struggle with tense feelings and the pervasive thoughts that no one else would understand. In reaching for perfectionistic ideals, you set up competitive dynamics with yourself and with others that make healthy relationships very difficult. Perfectionism tells you that you're striving for the best when what you're actually striving for is impossible—which is why you're constantly disappointed.

Building the habits and mindset to defeat impostor syndrome, including giving up perfectionism, can take time and repeated effort. But the rewards that this process can bring to your life are immeasurable, especially in teaching you to feel appreciation and compassion for yourself and others. Once you break the idea that you're only worthy when you're perfect, you learn that you're always worthy—when you're flawed, when you make mistakes, when you struggle. You're worthy! Breaking this perfection mythology is difficult, but it is possible. It's also a very important aspect of overcoming impostor syndrome, and it will give you more than you can even imagine.

TYPES OF PERFECTIONISM

Perfectionism is defined as always evaluating oneself with rigid personal standards that refuse to accept anything less than perfection. In their multidimensional model of perfectionism, Paul L. Hewitt and Gordon L. Flett describe three types of perfectionism:

Self-oriented: Having impossible expectations of yourself, placing an unreasonable level of importance on being perfect, and being overly critical in your self-evaluation of your performance.

Socially prescribed: Believing that your family, friends, and colleagues are extremely demanding and will judge you harshly if you're not perfect—and so you must be perfect in order to secure their approval.

Other-oriented: Requiring unattainable standards of others, and being highly critical of them.[10]

In their 2017 study, Thomas Curran and Andrew Hill found that recent generations of college students report higher levels of socially prescribed perfectionism than did previous generations—bringing the scholars to conclude that all three types of perfectionism have increased over a twenty-seven-year period (1989–2016).[11]

These findings suggest that individuals feel great societal pressure to meet unrealistic standards, which will ultimately lead to disappointment and frustration.

As you begin the process of working to give up perfectionism, consider the following questions:

Self-Oriented Perfectionism

- What is driving these unfair expectations of myself?
- Where do these high standards originate from?
- How can I be kinder to myself when setting expectations?
- What costs am I experiencing from self-oriented perfectionism?

Socially Prescribed Perfectionism

- What elements of my social context (e.g., family members, friends, social media) are driving my desire for perfectionism?

- What is my biggest fear regarding others' judgment of me? Has that fear ever actualized? If it has, does my perfectionism actually prevent it? Might there be other ways to look at or address the situation?

- How do I reduce the pressure I feel from socially prescribed perfectionism? How do I let myself not be perfect—be flawed—in social situations?

- The next time I appear flawed or make a mistake in a social situation, how can I approach myself with more compassion?

Other-Oriented Perfectionism

- From whom do I tend to demand perfection (e.g., children, colleagues, direct reports)? Why are they the particular targets? What is being evoked in me?

- How can I be kinder to them when setting expectations? What would it mean to set more reasonable expectations for them?

- What are the costs of my other-oriented perfectionism? Do I have strained relationships because of it?

- What would I like to see instead in these relationships?

EXERCISE 3.8: TYPES OF PERFECTIONISM

Describe which type of perfectionism is most prevalent for you and how it shows up in your life. (For example: socially prescribed—"I try to maintain a perfect image of my life on social media.")

_____

_____

_____

_____

_____

PERCEIVED BENEFITS OF PERFECTIONISM

Giving up perfectionism, even after defeating impostor syndrome, can be challenging due to the belief that there are perceived benefits to keeping it, such as higher levels of performance, greater motivation, more work engagement, and consistent work output.

Individuals who have perfectionistic tendencies worry that, without them, they would not be able to sustain their optimal levels of work performance. As a result, those perfectionistic tendencies may remain despite having overcome impostor syndrome. Interestingly, although research has found that perfectionists are more *motivated* on the job than those who are not perfectionists, there has been no link found between perfectionism and actual performance.[12] In other words, those perfectionistic notions did not result in a perfect or a better performance than those without perfectionistic tendencies.

Armed with the realization of this reality, can you think of ways to be motivated by things other than perfectionism? Can you allow yourself to replace the perfectionism motivator with something healthier for you? (Perhaps learning, enjoyment, or your own goals?)

EXERCISE 3.9: WHY I CAN'T GIVE UP PERFECTIONISM

Consider if there are perceived benefits of perfectionism that make it difficult for you to give it up. Are those benefits real? Is perfectionism the only way you can achieve those benefits? Might there be other choices for you that are healthier?

_____

_____

_____

_____

_____

COSTS OF PERFECTIONISM

While many may attribute their success to their perfectionism, those high standards have costs, such as: workaholism, anxiety and depression, high levels of stress and burnout, and strained relationships. And since we've established that perfectionism is not responsible for improved performance, it's hopefully evident to you that the perceived benefits of perfectionism do not outweigh its costs. It's not making you a better performer—and it's likely making you burned out, anxious, and stuck.

STEPS TO GIVING UP PERFECTIONISM

When your impostor syndrome is triggered, it is normal to feel a pull for perfectionism. If we feel we're not good enough—or a fraud—it's easy to imagine that trying to be perfect could remedy the situation. But those who have dealt with impostor syndrome know that the perfectionism never remedies the self-doubt. If anything, it makes it worse. So, let's talk about ways to give it up by taking some key steps.

Step 1: Acknowledge that perfectionism is not responsible for your success. As noted earlier, no link has been found between perfectionism and better performance. By acknowledging that it is your skills, your experience, and your talents that are responsible for your success, not perfection, it will be less challenging to give it up.

Step 2: Accept the fact that the perceived benefits of perfectionism do not outweigh its costs. As previously discussed, perfectionism leads to burnout and stress, anxiety and depression, interpersonal consequences, and other mental health effects—none of which is worth the perceived benefits of perfectionism.

Step 3: Embrace a growth mindset. The fear for many perfectionists is that making a mistake will result in not reaching prescribed goals or being exposed as a fraud or a failure. Even when you've conquered impostor syndrome, you may remain convinced that mistakes are unacceptable if you want to succeed in your career advancement. Consider instead embracing a growth mindset—a term coined by the psychologist Dr. Carol Dweck to describe a way of thinking that understands that intelligence is not finite, that people can improve through effort and hard work (not overwork), and that mistakes are in fact opportunities for growth.[13] If you embrace a growth mindset, you can approach learning with less perfectionistic tendencies and with decreased stress.

Step 4: Strive for greatness, not perfection. Giving up perfection does not mean that you will not continue to be ambitious and motivated to reach your goals. Rather, it calls for changing your mentality so that you are striving to be great or even just "good enough" in your endeavors—without having to be perfect.

Step 5: Seek support when your perfectionism and impostor syndrome are triggered. As we've noted, there may be situations (such as at a new job, or when meeting new people) where your impostor syndrome gets triggered, and you may feel pulled to reactivate your perfectionism.

Perfectionism can drive us to hide from others, but that prevents us from really getting what we need—community. Instead of lapsing back into perfectionism, it will be essential that you reach out to the mentors and colleagues in your Dream Team, requesting support during your current challenges. Note that it's especially difficult for leaders to admit that their impostor syndrome and perfectionism are being triggered and then to do something proactive about it, but it is imperative that you reach out for help, because your struggles may be affecting more than just you.

Breaking free of burnout practices and giving up perfectionism are key aspects of protecting your dream. Even after defeating impostor syndrome, you may continue to struggle with holding on to unhealthy and dysfunctional habits. By utilizing the strategies in this chapter, you can eliminate such behaviors, increase your overall well-being, and protect the dreams you've established on your path to a life free of impostor syndrome.

KEY TAKEAWAYS

In closing this chapter, we hope that:

- You recognize the causes of your burnout and how myths about burnout may sustain it.
- You've learned about burnout practices and how to reduce them.
- You understand the different types of perfectionism and their impact on your impostor syndrome.
- You've identified the costs/benefits of perfectionism.
- You've committed to giving up perfectionism and know the steps to take to do so.

PART TWO
ASSESSMENT

Chapter 4

ACKNOWLEDGING YOUR FIRST SYSTEM

As we enter this section of the book, we ask you to take a moment to reflect on what you've learned about yourself and who you want to be as you move forward. Once you've done that, we're going to explore in more detail what that future looks like in the context of systems and organizations that may not be supportive of your dreams and are therefore not set up for you to succeed. These systems want you to be in complete submission, to give more of yourself than is healthy, and to be a "good kid/employee." We're going to teach you how to be conscious of these systemic dynamics that once felt so oppressive and overwhelming. With that consciousness and perspective you'll be able to retain your sense of self and assess your path forward.

While you've done a lot of work on yourself, others around you, including the gatekeepers for these systems, have likely not done that work. We want to create opportunities for you to be at your optimum even in toxic, oppressive, and hostile systems. So we're going to show you how to maintain and even grow your effectiveness—and how to honor yourself and your ability to consistently own your greatness—no matter what you're having to deal with.

FAMILY SYSTEMS

We'll start with the first system you ever knew: your family. Family systems are where we first learn about authority, ourselves, and ourselves in relation to others. The family system is where boundaries are first taught—or not taught, as is usually the case for those of us who struggle with impostor syndrome. It's the system where you first interacted with peers—in this case your siblings, cousins, and friends. The family system demonstrated how conflict is managed—or not managed. It taught you how to behave when you had something to celebrate, and what to feel and do when you made a mistake. And it likely contributed to your developing impostor syndrome. The family system, in essence, is the foundation for our largely unconscious understanding of how to behave within an organization. In other words, we often make sense of our work systems by processing them through the lens of our early childhood—most times without even realizing that we're doing so.

In helping you actualize your greatness, we want to teach you to approach the difficult organizations that you will undoubtedly encounter in a new way. First, we need to consider what your family unit taught you about systems so we can identify what needs to be unlearned.

TWO TYPES OF SYSTEMS

A system is a group of interacting or interrelated elements that act according to a set of rules to form a unified whole.[14]

A family system is a group of interconnected family members. Systems theory suggests that human behavior within the family unit is a complex social system in which members interact to influence each other's behaviors. This interconnectedness views the family members in the system as a whole rather than as separate individuals.[15]

How we needed to function within the family provided the foundation for impostor syndrome—and that's the central reason we show up in our work systems endlessly trying to prove ourselves. And yet, the paradox is that those of us with impostor syndrome often feel destined to remain at the periphery of the systems we regularly participate in. We can be very loyal to these systems—work and family—but some of us never feel fully in the circle, and never feel seen for who we are. Another angle of this is that we can operate as lone wolves on the fringes of a system even if we're on a team. Sometimes, we feel safest and most protected when working alone. So, as we work on our impostor syndrome, it's incredibly important to our healing that we learn to trust systems again—at least the ones we consider psychologically safe. Once we learn to identify which systems to venture into—and attempt to successfully function within—it is a critical step for us to *choose* to truly belong.

In order to identify which systems are healthy and which are not, we need to better understand the dynamics of the first system that taught us to feel vulnerable: the family. So in this chapter we're going to dive deep into understanding some of the vulnerabilities of impostor syndrome. The purpose of this is to develop a lens with which to recognize and evaluate the most common unhealthy patterns that people with impostor syndrome are susceptible to. Once we learn how to see them with greater clarity, we can learn how to interact with them with greater agency.

CASE STUDY: LISA (continued from page 62)

Recently, Lisa was giving a talk for an organization that supports high-potential leaders. Someone during the Q&A asked: "Why are women such bad leaders? I've had several bad bosses in my career, and they've always been women." Now, as a diversity, equity, and inclusion consultant, Lisa has heard this kind of generalization before. But instead of replying as the questioner expected, Lisa asked her to reflect on her relationship with her mother (but without sharing that with the group). Lisa asked: "Did she show up in the ways that some of these difficult bosses have? Have you found peace and forgiveness in that relationship?" The questioner thought for a moment and then asked, "How did you know I had a difficult relationship with my mother?"—as if Lisa were a mind reader performing tricks at a fair. Lisa replied, "Because when we repeat a dynamic so repetitively, it's often because we haven't done the healing in a primary or foundational relationship—so that's why we keep repeating it." In other words, it was as if the initial question hadn't been "Why are women such bad leaders?" but "Why didn't my mother model leadership for me in a healthy way? And why do I keep looking for her (in the forms of these other bosses) to finally do that—when I know she can't since she doesn't have the skills?"

The phenomenon just described is called "repetition compulsion." It's a psychological concept that posits we will repeat unresolved, unhealthy dynamics from our childhood in the hope that something different and healthier will happen. The issue is, since the new people are very similar to the people in the earlier dynamic, the chances of there being a different outcome are very small. Breaking the repetition compulsion usually means doing some healing, ideally in a therapeutic context, regarding the person in the original dynamic. The goal is to accept that the original situation occurred as it did, forgive, and let it go. It also means looking with greater clarity at the present-day circumstances that trigger this repeating for you so that you can make different, healthier choices.

There are many unhealthy dynamics that can be toxic in systems. In this book, we'll largely focus on the two dynamics that are most commonly associated with impostor syndrome: codependent family dynamics and narcissistic caregiver dynamics. As you read further, consider how the dynamics compare with what you experienced in your early family life.

CODEPENDENT FAMILY DYNAMICS

When we struggle with impostor syndrome, particular dynamics from our childhood often unconsciously lead us to make certain decisions in our work life. For example, if you experienced codependent dynamics in your childhood, you might be pulled by leaders who speak of their team as a "family," who talk about doing "anything" for their work or team members, who may be crisis oriented, and/or who look for an employee who will "give their absolute all." You may be unconsciously enticed by certain personality types and cues that echo the type of family you grew up in—even if you hated it—if you haven't yet been able to process the original dynamic.

In these dynamics, you may find yourself attempting to be the "good kid or employee" trying to please your bosses/parents/authority figures and suppressing your own needs—even if those needs are crucial to your survival. This is because, in the earlier family dynamic, assessing and determining what others needed from you in order for them to be at *their* best was so foundational to your functioning that you lost complete sight of what you needed. Breaking these dynamics can be incredibly difficult because it's easy to feel that, if you stopped performing duties in support of those who depend on you, they wouldn't succeed (read: survive). That dynamic is the quintessential construct of codependent families.

CODEPENDENT FAMILY DYNAMICS

Codependent family dynamics can look like the following:

- The family is organized around ("overfunctions") a member struggling with physical or mental health, who typically "underfunctions." This can also be described in terms of "over-responsibility" for some and "under-responsibility" for others.
- A family member engages in self-sacrifice.
- There is inappropriate caretaking, such as a child looking after a parent.
- One or more family members consistently seeks the approval of others.
- One or more family members is unable to set boundaries—which can lead to overinvolvement in others' lives.

- One or more family members exhibits problematic behavior for which they are not held accountable.
- Family members have difficulty expressing emotion and dealing with conflict.
- One or more family members has trust issues with self and others.[16]

In a codependent family dynamic, your needs are subsumed under the needs of others. As a result, you take care of yourself only once every other need in the system has been met. Spelled out, that means you sacrifice well-being, health, your mental wellness, your needs, and your goals in service to anyone perceived to have a need greater than your own—which might be everyone. Putting yourself first can feel like a narcissistic venture, as though you were indifferent to the needs of those around you. However, what this self-assessment fails to acknowledge is that the people whose needs you constantly put first are often adults, and thus are completely capable of managing the tasks in their purview. By engaging in this way, we enable their supposed helplessness and support their incompetence—which both diminishes what they're truly capable of and requires us to always do more.

WEAPONIZED INCOMPETENCE

Definition: When a person pretends not to know how to complete a task, or exaggerates their inability to perform it, no matter how simple or complex, in order to shift the burden of responsibility to another.

But if you as an overfunctioning family member work to reduce that behavior, two positive outcomes can emerge. Ideally the shift can encourage the underfunctioning family members to live up to their full potential—though often they don't. But, regardless, that shifted dynamic can encourage *you* to prioritize your own needs. Getting out of the habit of overfunctioning on behalf of others can be a major step toward establishing appropriate boundaries for yourself.

Now, let's consider the ways in which you experienced codependent family dynamics.

EXERCISE 5.1: CODEPENDENT FAMILY DYNAMICS

For this first exercise, identify which of the following applied to your early family life.

❑ The family centered around a "designated patient."

❑ You were expected to minimize your needs, or manage them on your own.

❑ You were expected to squelch your emotions. For example, if you got upset when there was something else "more important" going on—which there usually was—you were expected to get over it or suck it up. In other words, there was no space for your emotions.

❑ Similarly, you were expected to be the "good kid" since they didn't need any more to deal with.

❑ Expressing contrary opinions—especially contrary to the older members of the family—was not supported or tolerated.

❑ It was hard, if not completely impossible, to change the way you engaged with the others in the family system.

EXERCISE 5.2: CODEPENDENT BOSSES OR ORGANIZATIONAL DYNAMICS

In this exercise, the goal is to see (first in general terms) how these codependent family dynamics can look in the workplace. Then, we want you to consider if/how each dynamic has played out in your work experience. If you are currently experiencing any of the following workplace dynamics, take some time to reflect on what it looks like for you. Putting words to these experiences can help to illustrate that which may have long been invisible.

Dynamic 1: We are a "family" or we are "friends."

How it looks/plays out: You can't set boundaries or ask for your needs to be met. You feel urged to self-sacrifice on behalf of your boss or the team.

Describe your experience with this, if any:

_____

_____

_____

Dynamic 2: Seek to all get along all the time.

How it looks/plays out: Your work environment screams "conflict avoidance": any interpersonal problems are ignored in favor of superficial demonstrations of "positive" culture.

Describe your experience with this, if any:

_____

_____

_____

Dynamic 3: You're in a closed system.

How it looks/plays out: It is as though no one is allowed to leave—unless the boss wants a change. Maintaining the status quo ensures that no new people, ideas, or change comes to the group; the team is stagnant. It also means you won't be looked upon kindly if you try to leave.

Describe your experience with this, if any:

_____

_____

_____

Dynamic 4: Boundaries are forbidden—either explicitly or implicitly; people-pleasing is central.

How it looks/plays out: Overworking or overfunctioning comes first; you can never prioritize meeting your own needs, especially if they would violate the group norms around work.

Describe your experience with this, if any:

_____

_____

_____

Dynamic 5: Feedback and criticism, especially of leaders, is not permitted.

How it looks/plays out: Though the leaders may say they're open to criticism, if you actually do critique anything, you're met with resistance.

Describe your experience with this, if any:

_____

_____

_____

Dynamic 6: All team members are required to tend to the boss's needs as a primary duty.

How it looks/plays out: The boss's needs are always most important. They are constantly monitored so as to ensure they are always pleased/satisfied. There is no room for your own needs or concerns.

Describe your experience with this, if any:

_____

_____

_____

Now, let's take a look at the other common family dynamic that shows up in the workplace—and that can play a significant role in impostor syndrome.

NARCISSISTIC CAREGIVER DYNAMICS

First, let's try to simply define what can be a confusing, complicated characteristic. In referring to "narcissism" we're generally referring to the narcissistic personality disorder. (But note: this could apply to someone without this diagnosis who is egotistical, self-centered, and/or arrogant.) Someone with narcissistic personality disorder is essentially blind to everyone else; no one else matters. Their needs and wants are central, and the people around them are utilized as merely instrumental (or not instrumental) to attain their goals. Worse yet, the narcissist tends to see others as an extension of themselves, without any regard for the other person's needs, wishes, emotions, boundaries, and own desires. This dynamic can be particularly distressing when the narcissist is a caregiver—usually a parent. Narcissistic caregivers tend to be emotionally or physically absent—which means the children don't receive the love, care, and attention they need.

ETYMOLOGY OF NARCISSISM

"Narcissism" gets its name from Narcissus in Greek mythology. Narcissus was a youth known for his beauty who fell in love with his own reflection in a pool of water. He remained there, transfixed, until he (according to most accounts) wasted away.[17]

Narcissistic caregiver dynamics can be particularly difficult to assess because often our love for our caregivers can create blind spots to their struggles. Narcissistic caregivers often developed this personality disorder because they themselves had narcissistic caregivers who were also absent. In a need to understand why they were not loved in the way that they needed, they inflate their value and how special they are. This inflated construction is very fragile and often referred to as a "house of cards." Just imagine: if the inflated construction is challenged by criticism, it can easily collapse—which is why narcissists fight criticism with aggressive tactics.

If you experienced a narcissistic caregiver, you may be drawn to work circumstances where the boss is seen as a sort of god. They may have a reputation in the field with many accolades and accomplishments—the kind of boss you should be elated to work for and so never complain about. They often surround themselves with people who idolize them and who never utter a word of dissent. You know why? Because that leader needs to remain at the top of the heap. You and your coworkers are just their minions. In this context, your own light will rarely if ever shine.

Working for narcissistic bosses can be incredibly difficult because if you attempt to challenge them you will experience severe consequences. They run the show, and you need to keep them happy. And so it can seem better to comply than to complain. However, the consequences of complying—of never expressing your own opinions or needs—are also great. So, once again, you're in an environment where you must ignore your own needs while being hypersensitive to others' needs.

Now, let's consider the ways in which you might have experienced narcissistic caregiver dynamics.

EXERCISE 5.3: NARCISSISTIC CAREGIVER DYNAMICS

Identify which of the following applied to your early family life.

❑ You were only pleasing if you succeeded at something one or more caregiver(s) deemed worthy.

❑ You were required to meet one or more caregiver(s)' needs and wishes.

❑ When you failed to meet expectations, you were subject to loss of love or attention.

❑ Your accomplishments, successes, and achievements were used to create visibility for one or more caregiver(s).

❑ If you critiqued or criticized your caregiver(s), they lashed out at you.

❑ If you made a mistake, it was met with a severe response or punishment.

EXERCISE 5.4: NARCISSISTIC BOSS DYNAMICS

With this exercise, the goal is to see (first in general terms) how narcissistic boss dynamics can look in the workplace. Then, we want you to consider if/how each dynamic has played out in your work experience. If you're currently experiencing any of the following workplace dynamics, take some time to reflect on what it feels like for you. Putting words to these experiences can help to illustrate that which may have long been invisible.

Dynamic 1: Your boss is not interested in knowing anything about you unless it relates to or benefits them. They see your advancement as a threat to them. They will cut you off if you leave their team.

How it looks/plays out: It's vividly clear: your role is to serve; you don't matter.

Describe your experience with this, if any:

_____

_____

_____

Dynamic 2: When you make a mistake, your boss personalizes it—seeing it as a reflection on them—and responds with hypercriticism and anger.

How it looks/plays out: Perfectionistic behavior is expected and reinforced.

Describe your experience with this, if any:

_____

_____

_____

Dynamic 3: When you give your boss feedback, they are fragile and reactive, and turn it back on you.

How it looks/plays out: They establish that they're beyond reproach.

Describe your experience with this, if any:

_____

_____

_____

Dynamic 4: Your boss creates fragmented teams that struggle to work together.

How it looks/plays out: A team with no cohesion isn't threatening—whereas a united team might rock the boat or mutiny.

Describe your experience with this, if any:

_____

_____

_____

Dynamic 5: Your boss needs to be front and center; they'll take credit for your work while minimizing you.

How it looks/plays out: Their performance and status is all that matters.

Describe your experience with this, if any:

_____

_____

_____

Dynamic 6: Your boss has no boundaries. When they need something, you are expected to sacrifice yourself for them.

How it looks/plays out: You are allowed no boundaries. You are at their beck and call.

Describe your experience with this, if any:

_____

_____

_____

Dynamic 7: The boss's needs are all that matter.

How it looks/plays out: Since there is no room for you to ask for help, there is no opportunity to get your needs met and to truly grow.

Describe your experience with this, if any:

_____

_____

_____

OTHER TOXIC BEHAVIORAL DYNAMICS

Though we've focused on the above dynamics, there are additional family dynamics that commonly contribute to impostor syndrome as well. Let's explore if you've experienced any of these dynamics.

EXERCISE 5.5: OTHER FAMILY DYNAMICS

Identify if any of the following applied to your early family life.

❑ Anger and conflict were not well managed in your family.

❑ Sibling competition was never addressed or managed.

❑ Family members had to follow strict rules in order to meet the parent(s)' expectations. Any misbehavior was punished.

❑ Pleasing others was considered paramount.

❑ People or situations were viewed in black and white, with no complexity.

❑ It was important to be considered the "hardworking one" or the "intelligent one."

❑ You didn't feel supported.

EXERCISE 5.6: OTHER TOXIC BEHAVIORAL DYNAMICS

Again, with this exercise the goal is to see (first in general terms) how these additional toxic dynamics can look in the workplace. Then, we want you to consider if/how each dynamic has played out in your work experience. If you're currently experiencing any of the following workplace dynamics, take some time to reflect on what it feels like for you. Putting words to these experiences can help to illustrate that which may have long been invisible.

Dynamic 1: Conflict is always avoided.

How it looks/plays out: Toxic behavior is allowed to continue unabated.

Describe your experience with this, if any:

_____

_____

_____

Dynamic 2: The work culture is one of people-pleasing/acquiescence.

How it looks/plays out: You have trouble saying "no" and setting boundaries. Because of this, you also have trouble knowing what you want for yourself, or even investing energy in finding out.

Describe your experience with this, if any:

_____

_____

_____

Dynamic 3: The work culture prioritizes intelligence above all else.

How it looks/plays out: You strive to outperform everyone at work and be valued for your "smarts"—to the extent that you struggle tremendously when you make a mistake or "under" perform.

Describe your experience with this, if any:

_____

_____

_____

Dynamic 4: The work culture prioritizes hard work/extreme effort above all else.

How it looks/plays out: You overwork, believing that putting in excessive hours is the only way to keep failure at bay.

Describe your experience with this, if any:

_____

_____

_____

Dynamic 5: Feeling expected to be the "survivor" on the team.

How it looks/plays out: People who felt they needed to keep the family together tend to be overly loyal to organizations and bosses. It's easy to desperately fear failing (the team) out of the concept that failure would be catastrophic. This focus is so prevalent that you don't recognize that your skills, experience, and expertise speak for themselves—you don't need to keep earning your place.

Describe your experience with this, if any:

_____

_____

_____

Dynamic 6: Rigid rules are the norm.

How it looks/plays out: You are very compliant. You would never assert any needs that go against the organization's expectations (read: "rules").

Describe your experience with this, if any:

_____

_____

_____

First, take a moment to congratulate yourself on the hard work you just did striving to gain clarity on what can be insidious environmental and interpersonal dynamics. This is no small feat! This capped the internal work of striving to unlock your greatness. Your job now is to work with the external world that seeks to reinforce (or restore) your impostor syndrome. Part of the next level of your work will be keying into the unhealthy dynamics that repeat themselves in your current life. Becoming aware of them and making conscious choices to not engage them—or to engage them differently—will be the next, powerful phase of overcoming your impostor syndrome.

As psychologists, we always talk about "making the unconscious conscious." This is our first step of behavioral change—because if you don't know it, or can't see it, you can't change it. So it's critical to see how your early family dynamics, the ones that created your impostor syndrome, show up in your current work life. That's why we had you look at some of the family dynamics that commonly create impostor syndrome to help you identify the ones that are central for you.

The purpose of reviewing those dynamics is to locate if you're still connected to them or whether you've been able to distance yourself from them and move on. So, as you begin to contemplate how impostor syndrome shows up for you at work, pay attention to the dynamics you recognized in the earlier exercises. Similarly, as you work on the following exercises, consider if anything reminds you of your family dynamics. You may learn something new.

REMEMBER YOUR DREAM TEAM

You'll recall that one of the central members of your Dream Team is a therapist. If reading this chapter—or any part of this book—leaves you feeling raw and vulnerable in a way that prevents you from moving forward in your work, consider reconnecting with your therapist, or setting out to find one. (For more on how to find a therapist, see Chapter 9 of *Own Your Greatness.*) Therapy can be crucial in moving your impostor syndrome work forward.

When you identify these family dynamics, notice if the correlated work behaviors are still active for you. Are you having trouble moving beyond these dynamics at work? If you are, it likely means this is an area you need to work on—perhaps with a therapist. Trying new behaviors can be especially difficult if you're haunted by the ghosts of your family past. Or perhaps you feel ready but you just don't know what behaviors to try. If this is currently the case for you, now is a good time to consult a career coach (also part of the Dream Team).

What's important to know is that a system does not have to dictate your behavior. You can make other choices—even if the system doesn't want you to. A person can change a system, but they never do it alone. You have to find a similarly minded community that can help you disrupt the toxic and dysfunctional behavior of that system. There's a moment like this in the 1960 movie *Spartacus*. The film was inspired by a historical figure from antiquity, Spartacus, a slave who led a revolt and escaped. In an iconic scene, Spartacus is being sought—amid a huge crowd—by Roman leaders set on punishing his revolt and returning him to slavery. Everyone in the crowd shouts out: "I'm Spartacus!" Often in oppressive systems, the leaders in the system try to make an example of a "scapegoat"—which according to Dictionary.com is "a person or group made to bear the blame for others or to suffer in their place." But this tactic is weakened when many side with the "scapegoat." Community is incredibly important to making change in a system.

THE CONTAINER AND HOW TO BREAK IT

"Group as a whole" theory (where the power of the system is thought to be at times more powerful than individual intent and behavior) has some critical concepts that are relevant to the process of breaking through toxic system behaviors. One of them is the idea of "the container." Within a system you can sometimes be pulled to "contain" a certain competency, experience, or behavior. For example, you may be forced to "contain" diversity in your organization because you're the only person from a diverse group. So, any time someone is offensive, or diversity issues are not considered, you're expected to bring these issues up and address them—even though everyone in the organization should be responsible for this behavior. One of the most powerful ways to change the role of being a container is by recognizing that you're in this role and deciding to relinquish it or delegate it among many others.

CASE STUDY: AFIYA

Afiya had always been the "smart" one in her household; as a result of being assigned that role, she took care of everything—from managing her mother's finances to helping her brother with his homework. She took up that role in every corner of her life as well. While working on her impostor syndrome, she recognized that she was "containing" intelligence and competence at home and at work, and she was tired of it. More than tired—she was exhausted, and constantly burned out. So she decided to stop overfunctioning in this way and share this role with others so they could believe in their own competence. And so, the next time her brother wanted her to review his history paper due the next day, instead of staying up late guiding him in improving it—and then being exhausted at work the next day—she said, "I trust you. You can handle this." In the end, this wasn't just a triumph for Afiya in moving away from containing this role; her brother did very well with his paper too, and told her he was very proud of himself. This positive outcome served as great encouragement for Afiya in continuing to let go of that container role.

The same can be said in the reverse. Perhaps someone in your work life serves as the container for vulnerability or need for support. Because of this, coworkers rush to their aid, providing all they need to get their work done—but in the end no one else gets any support. So if you were struggling with your own work, you could help to shift the container by requesting help yourself. You could also help shift it by trusting this colleague to be able to handle their own workload and not volunteering to help them before they ask. And then, when they do ask, another shift could be to help them with guidance and instruction—but leaving them to do the actual work.

EXERCISE 5.7: WHO IS SERVING AS A CONTAINER?

Take a moment to consider if you're serving as a container in your personal and work life. Do other people over-rely on you? Do they under-rely on you? How might you work to shift this container role?

Also think about if any of the people in your personal and work life might be acting as a container, and how you might work to share in that.

_____

_____

_____

_____

_____

Working on changing containment issues in work and family life is one way to break up the rigid roles that are such a central part of impostor syndrome. Noticing when you and others get stuck as the container can be helpful in creating more varied and whole experiences for yourself and others. It's critical to break the way that we have often been seen—and see ourselves—when we are so much more than that.

KEY TAKEAWAYS

In closing this chapter, we hope that:

- You understand how our early family experiences can leave us vulnerable to dynamics that can lead to impostor syndrome.
- You've determined if the dynamics described in the exercises apply to your early family life—and, if so, that you have put these dynamics into words.
- You've considered if some dynamics from your family life are playing out in your workplace as well—and, if so, that you have put these dynamics into words.
- You have an understanding of the concept of containment and how you can work to shift it so as to help yourself and others to think outside that limited box.

Chapter 5

MANAGING TOXIC CULTURES

In the previous chapter, we discussed how your childhood family sets up expectations about systems—and how, when we have impostor syndrome, we may head into our work lives with systems templates that are unhealthy for us. In this chapter, we'll discuss how to recognize elements of toxic work cultures and their links to family dynamics, as well as how to manage them in order to increase your career success and satisfaction.

IDENTIFYING ELEMENTS OF TOXIC WORK CULTURES

No workplace culture is perfect. However, there's a difference between a lackluster yet functional work culture and a toxic, dysfunctional work culture. But if you're familiar with what to look for, you'll be able to recognize the warning signs early, and can make sure you escape a toxic work environment that would have adversely impacted your career satisfaction and success. A 2022 study in *MIT Sloan Management Review* found that a toxic work culture is "10.4 times more powerful than compensation in predicting a company's attrition rate, compared with its industry."[18] According to this study, toxic work culture included failure to promote diversity, equity, and inclusion; workers feeling disrespected; and unethical behavior. Their point being, companies who believe that raising compensation solves for retention miss the point of what is really driving attrition.

CASE STUDY: SIMONE

Simone had worked as an assistant editor for a lifestyle magazine for three years. Her work was very intense, and her office culture made it more difficult. For example, she constantly felt undermined by cutthroat competition. There were poor boundaries, where everyone felt on call 24/7. There was a culture of "stars and scapegoats." And as the only African American woman on the team, she was constantly exposed to microaggressions—plus there was clearly a disregard for diversity, equity, and inclusion. Although she enjoyed her work responsibilities, Simone sought our services because she wanted to leave her toxic work culture.

There are several elements to recognize as part of a toxic work culture:

Overwork is the norm and is rewarded: As we've discussed, hard work is needed for any job, and most people are not opposed to it. However, overwork, where you're working a disproportionate number of hours—late hours, on the weekends, on holidays and/or vacations—is an indicator of a toxic work environment. Unfortunately, for many industries (such as finance, management consulting, and corporate law), overwork is viewed as simply a normal part of the work culture and a badge of honor. The senior leaders in these fields have no incentive to change, as they believe that the prestige of the role will continue to attract incredibly intelligent and talented people—while keeping their clients, who are accustomed to around-the-clock service, happy. Such a dynamic is evident where it's the employees who don't mind working sixty-to-one-hundred-hour weeks who typically get the best case assignments—and eventually promoted to partner.

The "stars" and "scapegoats" dynamic: In a dysfunctional organization, employees see each other sectioned into groups of stars and scapegoats. Neither position feels very safe. If you're a star, you feel you must maintain stellar work or you'll fall from grace—and may become a scapegoat. If you're a scapegoat you're considered a failure, and no one is inclined to help you develop as an employee. Worse yet, leaders consider scapegoats as deserving the label—rather than considering what mechanism within the organization could develop employees who are struggling.

Poor boundaries: Another sign of a toxic work culture is the expectation that you be accessible 24/7 with no regard for your time boundaries; where meetings are put on your calendar without consultation or an agenda; and where your priorities can be derailed at any time by someone else's emergency. You tend to feel no sense of control over your time or your workflow.

"Othering" in the workplace: A lack of diversity, equity, and inclusion contributes to a toxic workplace. When you're labeled as a "diversity hire" because you come from a marginalized group (e.g., BIPOC, women), the unspoken intention implies that you weren't hired for your qualifications—you were solely hired for your marginalized group identity, which is a sign of toxicity. "Othering" in the workplace means that those who don't fit the perceived norm (e.g., White, cisgender, heterosexual male) are marginalized, do not have equitable access to career advancement opportunities, experience more incidents of bias, and do not have a sense of belonging to the company. You always feel different—like "the other."

Ineffective diversity, equity, and inclusion (DEI) initiatives: As mentioned earlier, failure to promote diversity, equity, and inclusion is one of the major signs of a toxic workplace, and a primary reason for attrition. When leaders of an organization ignore calls for a more diverse workforce, only include their favorites for prized opportunities—excluding most others—and offer no equitable access to growth opportunities, it is clear there are DEI concerns. However, there's another dynamic at play, one that is not often addressed: when the DEI initiatives place more burden on the very employees they're supposed to help. For instance, oftentimes many DEI leadership programs mandate additional work from their marginalized workforce—such as volunteering them for DEI Councils, task forces, and to head Employee Resource Groups (ERGs)—with no accommodation made to their job duties and schedules; with no additional compensation for the additional hours, which forces the employees to overwork to meet all expectations; and, to top it off, with no discernible career advancement opportunities tangibly resulting from this participation. Worse yet, participation in DEI initiatives such as DEI Executive Leadership Programs, DEI Councils, ERGs, and affinity groups can result in burnout *and* lower ratings on performance reviews for the role in which they are actually compensated.

Unhealthy competition: We recognize that a little bit of competition can actually be motivating, especially in industries like sales. However, when the level of competition makes it impossible to trust your colleagues or your boss—because you regard each other as the "enemy" or a threat—the competition is unhealthy.

Manipulative and bullying management: Another aspect of toxic work cultures is when employees feel disrespected, threatened, harassed, or otherwise under duress. One way this happens is when they are managed through manipulation and bullying. An example of this would be a supervisor not providing a formal performance review to employees, telling them they must figure out their growth areas on their own. The manager's intention here is to encourage employees to constantly prove themselves in all aspects of their work. Of course the prevalence of workplace bullying varies, but some studies indicate that 49 percent of employees report being either a target or a witness to bullying—demonstrating it's a major problem. Further, it's clear that a fair portion of this toxicity derives from management; the Workplace Bullying Institute reports from a survey that 65 percent of bullies were bosses.[19]

Arbitrary (or nonexistent) performance review processes: Some organizations pride themselves on being "up or out" organizations—meaning if you don't meet a particular performance cutoff you'll be asked to leave, even if you're still performing well. The late Jack Welch, General Electric's former CEO, was famous for discussing his "10 percent" rule, where he directed his leaders to eliminate the bottom 10 percent of employees in their work units every year. This process, called forced ranking or "rank and yank," was designed to improve the quality of the workforce by weeding out the lowest-performing team members. While to some that may seem fair in theory, it often pits employees against each other, creates a culture of fear, and allows bias and discrimination to taint the evaluation process.[20]

In contrast, some organizations have no performance review process, leaving employees constantly on edge about how they're progressing in the company, with no opportunity or process to understand how to improve. Both styles of performance review process can contribute to a toxic work culture. Thankfully, many companies have moved away from forced ranking in favor of continuous feedback and coaching/training.

EXERCISE 5.1: IDENTIFYING ELEMENTS OF YOUR TOXIC WORK CULTURE

Identify all the elements of toxic work cultures that currently exist in your workplace.

❑ Overwork is rewarded

❑ Stars and scapegoats

❑ Poor boundaries

❑ "Othering"

❑ Management by manipulation

❑ Bullying

❑ Unhealthy competition

❑ Ineffective diversity, equity, and inclusion initiatives

❑ Arbitrary/nonexistent performance review processes

THE DANGER OF THE "WE ARE A FAMILY" PARADIGM TO A HEALTHY WORK CULTURE

Another of the more toxic aspects of a work culture is when a boss or an organization talks up the concept of the team being a "family." While initially such a term may conjure notions of warmth, unconditional love, and connections sustained over a lifetime, there are a variety of issues at hand. First, it sets up employees to feel they must always put the needs of the "family" first, instead of considering their own concerns—such as finding a job that treats them better.

Second, leaders often say this to create an automatic sense of closeness and loyalty to the organization without actually producing behavior that would engender trust and connectedness. Unfortunately, many leaders may develop their leadership style from their own challenging dynamics within their families of origin, which they then dysfunctionally enact with their team members.

Overall, the "we are a family" paradigm can create unhealthy dynamics such as:

Codependence: Codependence is when an employee feels so connected to the organization that they're unable to separate their own needs from those of the organization. For instance, some of our clients have discussed feeling guilty about considering leaving a toxic work situation due to fear that they'll let down their team members or that their boss will get angry. Such feelings are tied to dysfunctional "family" dynamics wherein you don't have the right to make your own decisions, especially if they're not aligned with what the organizational "family" wants.

Splitting: Splitting is when a leader sees things dichotomously: using black-and-white thinking (e.g., that team members are "all good" or "all bad") depending on their perceived performance from moment to moment. Such splitting can occur with an insecure or narcissistic boss who is unable to view things or people with greater nuance.

Triangulation: Triangulation, which is a form of splitting, occurs when a person (usually a supervisor) attempts to manipulate through exclusion or by dividing and conquering. Typically, triangulation pits a pair of individuals or a larger group against a single person or a smaller group—creating a "triangle" of two against one. For example, the boss might attempt to create unhealthy competition by blatantly playing favorites to make team members jealous of and wary of each other. This is similar to a family dynamic where a caregiver instigates siblings competing for their love, pitting them against each other by talking about them behind their backs.

Development of fixed roles: With this dynamic, employees are placed in fixed informal roles—the smart one, the hardworking one, the incompetent one, the trusted ally, etc.—that keep them stuck in the same position with no opportunity for growth. At worst, the fixed role stunts professional development and/or self-esteem. Since these fixed roles in early childhood tend to contribute to the origins of impostor syndrome, they can continue impostor syndrome in the workplace.

Poor boundaries: We noted earlier how poor boundaries can lead to the expectation that you can be accessed 24/7. An additional angle of that in the "we are family" paradigm concerns the boss divulging personal information that you might not want to share in—and then perhaps expects you to do the same in return. Often this practice is used to make you feel like you're in the inner circle—essentially to create forced intimacy—but sometimes that personal information can be held against you. For example, let's say your boss has been treating you poorly and yelling at you in meetings—but then calls you into her office to tell you she's having marital problems, sharing details that make you uncomfortable and that make it hard for you to address how her behavior is affecting you.

Persistence of and tolerance for abusive treatment: In some families, a particular family member can be verbally abusive, make a scene when they're angry, and so on—and then simply apologize for their outbursts, time and time again, with no ill consequences (for them). Therefore, if a boss or a colleague demonstrates such behavior in a workplace where it's stated that "we are a family," it's considered perfectly fine for them to just apologize and move on— and then do it again. It's not reported to human resources or addressed because, as the thinking goes, "that's just what families do." But no matter how frustrated or angry someone may be, in no circumstance is it acceptable to throw things; yell; berate, stonewall, or gossip about a coworker; or be emotionally or physically abusive to your coworkers in any way (including making them feel excluded, calling them names, etc.). If an outburst occurs and a sincere apology is given, followed with behavioral change, then that single outburst can be forgiven. But there should be zero tolerance for a pattern of abusive or bullying behavior in the workplace.

EXERCISE 5.2: EXAMINING THE "WE ARE A FAMILY" DYNAMIC

Does the "we are a family" paradigm impact your impostor syndrome? Does it impact your functioning in the workplace? Describe your experience.

_____

_____

_____

_____

WHY VIEWING YOUR COLLEAGUES AS FAMILY CAN BE DETRIMENTAL

When you're struggling with impostor syndrome, it can feel like the only way to be successful is by pleasing others. So, if you're told that your work organization is like a family, you might be inspired to do everything in your power to make the family happy—essentially to *stay* in the family. Unfortunately, this mindset can have many negative consequences, such as what follows:

- It can give you a false sense of security, leading you to believe your job will always be safe and discouraging you from striving for better opportunities.

- It can make you more tolerant of toxic behavior based on the assumption that every family has some.

- It can make it difficult or impossible to maintain appropriate work boundaries, with your job consuming your life and adversely impacting your relationships outside of work. And it can make you feel compelled to share details about your personal life—and to hear details about your coworkers' lives, even if you're uncomfortable doing so.

- It can give you feelings of guilt due to an outsized loyalty to the organization or your boss that might not be reciprocated.

- It can make you reluctant to leave your position out of fear that you'll be cut off from the work "family."

CASE STUDY: LAURIE

Laurie worked for a research institute within a team of nine members. Her boss was always saying they were family, and the team routinely celebrated birthdays and had frequent after-work outings. However, Laurie had become increasingly uncomfortable with her boss's demands, including that she disclose information about her dating life. Her boss also tended to call or text her on weekends, often discussing her impending divorce or requesting that Laurie do small errands for her on her way to work, like picking up dry cleaning or returning a gift. Laurie also didn't like when her boss gossiped to her about other team members. Laurie sought our services to figure out how to handle such a challenging boss. She was also concerned about her boss's response if she were to find a new job, because her boss had totally ignored a team member and made them miserable after they resigned and gave two-weeks' notice. This fear made it difficult for Laurie to focus on a job search.

In an unhealthy "we are family" dynamic, you may feel reluctant or guilty about seeking a different position due to concerns about the response you'll get; perhaps you fear you'll be ostracized, or your boss will express feelings of abandonment or betrayal. When our clients express such feelings, we typically note that a healthy, truly supportive colleague or boss would be happy for you to pursue a better opportunity. While they may be disappointed and sad that you're leaving, if they cut you off or demonstrate feelings of anger toward you, it's evidence of an unhealthy "we are a family" dynamic.

YOUR OPTIONS WHEN DEALING WITH A TOXIC WORK CULTURE

When you've experienced impostor syndrome, being in a toxic work setting can constantly trigger and sustain it. You may feel stuck and believe that you don't have any options. But you actually have several options, including building alliances and being strategic in how you manage these interactions—as well as considering options outside your current workplace.

BUILDING ALLIANCES

When you're dealing with impostor syndrome in a toxic work culture, you may believe you're alone in your experience. Sadly, such environments may cause you to feel extremely distrustful of your colleagues, making you less likely to confide in them. However, one of the most important strategies to combating impostor syndrome is to build alliances. As we noted before, having a Dream Team is crucial to defeating impostor syndrome. We all need support in internalizing our unique talents and skills. We encourage you to seek out allies who will support your efforts and will enable you to support theirs in turn. For starters, you and your allies can help each other recognize the following about a toxic work environment:

- Overwork should not be the norm.
- Perfection should not be the goal.
- Self-care is an important part of career success and satisfaction.
- People-pleasing to the detriment of your needs is unhealthy.
- Having strong boundaries is a key component of good self-care practice.
- You're not alone.

Furthermore, work allies can also possibly help you to change the toxic work culture so you can all have a healthier and happier work experience. (We'll cover strategic options for managing difficult and toxic work environments in greater detail in later chapters.)

EXERCISE 5.3: FINDING ALLIES

Identify current or potential allies in your workplace. Describe how they can support you in reducing your impostor feelings and countering your toxic work culture.

_____

_____

_____

EXPLORING OTHER OPTIONS

When you have impostor syndrome, it's easy to believe you're not good enough to find better work options. While having allies is important, in order to push back against or even to change the culture, at a certain point it may be time to move on.

EXERCISE 5.4: COPING WITH TOXIC WORK ENVIRONMENTS

Describe how you currently deal with your toxic work culture. Do you tend to overwork? Do you try to just ignore it? (Perhaps refer back to your replies to Exercise 3.5: Burnout Practices on page 60.)

_____

_____

Consider how you could deal with it in a healthier way. Perhaps build alliances, explore other options.

_____

_____

EXERCISE 5.5: WHAT'S KEEPING YOU STUCK?

If you're considering other options, explore what factors may be keeping you stuck (e.g., fear, financial considerations, family of origin dynamics, etc.).

Toxic bosses and toxic work cultures play major roles in sustaining impostor syndrome. As you come to own your greatness, it will be important to also identify the elements of a toxic work culture, which can continue to trigger your impostor syndrome, so that you can develop a plan of action to live a healthier and more satisfying work life.

KEY TAKEAWAYS

In closing this chapter, we hope that:

- You've learned how to identify the typical elements of toxic work cultures.
- You understand how dysfunctional family dynamics can contribute to toxic work cultures.
- You recognize why the "we are a family" paradigm at work can be harmful to you.
- You're starting to consider your options in countering a toxic workplace. This includes committing to identifying both all the ways you can cope as well as what might be keeping you stuck.
- You're committed to identifying allies in the workplace to help counter your toxic work culture.

Chapter 6

IDENTIFYING TOXIC LEADERSHIP

When we struggle with impostor syndrome, bosses, mentors, leaders, and authority figures are central to how we conceptualize ourselves, our success, our progress, and our future. Breaking free from impostor syndrome means reevaluating and restructuring this relationship with authority. Rather than having this relationship dictate how you feel about yourself and what you want for yourself, you'll want to consider *if* this relationship with authority assists you in reaching your dreams and goals—and then commit accordingly. When we've experienced impostor syndrome, we typically have always felt subordinate or subservient to authority. In this chapter, we'll discuss how to change this paradigm and instead develop a healthy, productive relationship to authority.

EARLY EXPERIENCES OF PARENTING STYLES AND AUTHORITY

It's probably no surprise to you at this point in the book that your template for authority comes from your experience with your parents and caregivers. They taught you how they expected and desired you to interact with them, and that practice formed the foundation of how you later interacted with bosses, mentors, and other leaders. There are three different styles of parenting, one or more of which can be experienced in a caregiving unit: authoritarian, permissive, and authoritative. Each of these leadership styles affects the way children develop a sense of self, self-direction, and ability to make decisions.

"Authoritarian" parenting figures lead through strict, dominant rule. What they say goes, and there is no space for challenge. They set extremely high expectations with little consideration for the child's capacity or developmental stage. They focus on discipline, obedience, and control rather than nurturing and building a relationship with their unique child. They expect the child not to make mistakes and to obey them. They usually provide only negative feedback, often in the form of punishment, for misbehavior or unmet expectations. They rarely provide positive feedback. They are very demanding, and they often micromanage every part of the child's life. They have a lot of rules but don't necessarily communicate them all. The child is left to try to figure them out—or else is punished for violating them. Punishments can be harsh and swift, and can be administered seemingly out of context. Such parents are often not responsive to the child's needs; they're often distant and emotionally unavailable, and are more likely to yell, chastise, or criticize than to compliment, engage, and explore. They often obtain compliance via dealing out shame and criticism in statements like, "What's wrong with you?" and "Why can't you do anything right?"

If this sounds familiar, it's because the authoritarian is the most common parenting style of people who suffer from impostor syndrome. Research shows that children raised in this type of parenting style can experience or exhibit the following:

- Be fearful and shy around others.
- Be overly concerned about what others think about them.
- Have trouble with decision-making.
- Associate obedience and success with love.
- Conform easily, and readily engage in people-pleasing behaviors.
- Experience depression and anxiety.
- Have low self-esteem.
- Have trouble setting limits and developing their own standards and values.[21]

As you can likely see, these are many of the same things that people with impostor syndrome experience and contend with, especially if you've been in the role of the "intelligent one" or the "hardworking one."

There are two other parenting styles that we'll discuss briefly. "Permissive" parents are often very nurturing; they also can expect very little from the child. In these relationships, the parent may behave (and seem) more like a friend than a parent. This is more like the "helicopter parent" who strives to protect the child from any hardship. They often use bribery to get a child to behave. They tend not to reinforce any rules or types of behaviors, and they provide little structure or schedule. Children raised in this type of parenting style can experience or exhibit the following:

- Be low achievers.
- Be poor decision-makers.
- Be unable to manage their time and habits.
- Show less emotional intelligence.

It's common to see families with one authoritarian parent or caregiver and the other a permissive parent as a counterbalance.

The final style is "authoritative." It's the healthiest style of parenting and unfortunately the one that readers of this book likely haven't seen in our childhoods—but should be aiming to model as parents, and should seek out in bosses or mentors. Authoritative parents listen to the child and are responsive to their needs. They may have high expectations of the child, but they also provide the resources and support needed to help the child succeed. They tend to provide love and warmth, as well as boundaries and discipline. They avoid punishments, bribes, or threats; instead, they reinforce constructive behavior and attempt to explore problematic behavior, knowing there must be an underlying cause that needs to be understood. They allow their child to express their own opinions. Their parenting style is flexible; they comprehend that each child and situation is unique, and that the child's development must be tailored to the child's unique needs and circumstances. Research shows that children with authoritative parents tend to experience or exhibit the following:

- Be self-confident about their ability to learn new things and function in new circumstances.
- Develop good social skills.
- Be good at regulating their emotions.
- Be content and satisfied with their lives.[22]

As you can see, this type of parenting style leads to healthy outcomes. Mentors and bosses with this style tend to be excellent at developing those they work with.

EXERCISE 6.1: PARENTING STYLE ASSESSMENT

Consider your own experience with parenting styles.

Caregiver name: _____

Parenting style (e.g., authoritarian, permissive, authoritative):_____

What was your experience with this parenting style?

_____

_____

_____

How does this parenting style show up in your life today?

_____

_____

_____

Caregiver name: _____

Parenting style (e.g., authoritarian, permissive, authoritative):_____

What was your experience with this parenting style?

_____

_____

_____

How does this parenting style show up in your life today?

_____

_____

_____

Caregiver name: _____

Parenting style (e.g., authoritarian, permissive, authoritative):_____

What was your experience with this parenting style?

_____

_____

_____

How does this parenting style show up in your life today?

_____

_____

_____

Another important piece around the concept of authority is the idea of authorizing and deauthorizing someone. "Authorizing" means giving someone permission to lead you, and "deauthorizing" means not giving (or rescinding) that permission. As we move toward learning how to choose the right authority figures in our lives, we need to pay greater attention to how we authorize and deauthorize leaders around us, as well as to whom we give authority. When we struggle with impostor syndrome, we tend to authorize anyone in a leadership role without question; we also tend to automatically deauthorize ourselves. This amounts to relinquishing our own power, strength, and influence, which puts us at a deficit.

EXERCISE 6.2: IDENTIFYING AUTHORIZING BEHAVIORS

Sometimes authorizing someone in a leadership role—such as a boss, teacher, or mentor—can lead to a healthy relationship that benefits us. Unfortunately, sometimes granting that authorization can lead to a detrimental relationship that harms us, especially if we unnecessarily deauthorize our own authority. In this exercise, we want you to identify and then examine the authorizing and deauthorizing behaviors you engage in. In the lists to follow, check any behaviors that apply.

Authorizing Behaviors

❑ Following orders or executing requests without questioning them.

❑ Looking for validation from those who are senior to you.

❑ Letting those you admire dictate your career path.

❑ Assuming you can trust a person entirely on account of their position or title—without evidence.

❑ Supporting someone else's advancement through your work.

❑ Being deferential in decision-making.

❑ Seeking to please leaders at all costs.

Deuthorizing Behaviors

❑ Dismissing or relinquishing your power in a particular situation.

❑ Dismissing compliments or positive feedback.

❑ Paying no attention to what *you* want in a situation.

❑ Not voicing your concerns or differences of opinion.

❑ Failing to celebrate your own wins and accomplishments.

❑ Not considering your own needs in decision-making.

❑ Not taking visible leadership.

EXERCISE 6.3: RETHINKING AUTHORIZING BEHAVIORS

Based on your replies to the above checklists, consider how you might concretely transform any authorizing behaviors that harm you into behaviors that would benefit you.

_____

_____

_____

_____

_____

LEADERSHIP REDEFINED

The discussion of parenting styles and authority naturally takes us to the subject of leadership. Our experience of parenting generates our connection to and relationship with leadership. As we move away from our impostor syndrome, we want to recharacterize the kind of leadership we want to affiliate with. Rather than believing we have no options, we want to realize that we do: we can choose leaders—bosses, mentors, teachers—who employ a healthy style of leadership. Those choice points can come to us in all kinds of moments. We can consider the potential boss's leadership style when we're looking for a new job or when we're asked to transfer to another team. Even when it seems like we have no choice—for example, if we already have a toxic boss, or if a new boss replaces our established boss—it's critical to remember that we can choose *how* we engage with this toxic boss, and how strong of a boundary we maintain between them and our experience, sense of self, and inner world.

Leadership is the process by which someone influences and supports others in delivering on specific organizational goals. This process encompasses both strategy and the management of people. A leader employing a healthy, constructive style of leadership considers how both organizational and individual goals can align so that, as the business grows, the people who are supporting it grow as well. A wise leader models the behavior they want to see in the people they influence. This leader thoughtfully considers both their actions and the implications of their actions on the business and the employees.

The above description is our view as executive coaches. Unfortunately, for far too long leaders have been expected to solely focus on the goals of the business, regardless of the workers who support that business. Indeed, toxic leaders function from the mindset of business *over* people. If you're a healthy leader, the people always come first. All the great leaders we've experienced or worked for have had this philosophy, and have run incredibly successful teams and organizations.

There are many ways to lead, and leadership comes at every level. You don't have to have the title of manager or a C-suite title to lead. There is both formal and informal leadership, and they derive their authority from different sources. Formal leadership is when you're officially recognized through your title and the scope of your role to manage a certain purview for the organization. Formal leaders derive their authority from their title and the hierarchy of that organization—as well as from employees' respect for that title and hierarchy. Informal leadership is when someone not holding a title or hierarchy is nonetheless seen to be influential in the group or organization. Informal leaders tend to be experienced, knowledgeable, strategic, and effective at managing their influence. Informal leaders derive their authority from trust, relationships, and reputation, as well as the qualities that others admire about them. Informal leaders can make a huge impact through their spheres of influence. As you can imagine, ideally those in a formal leadership role lead with both formal and informal leadership styles.

STRATEGIES OF INFLUENCE

The Center for Creative Leadership discusses three strategic ways to influence an organization.[23]

Influencing with Head, Heart, and Hands

LOGICAL APPEALS (HEAD)	EMOTIONAL APPEALS (HEART)	COOPERATIVE APPEALS (HANDS)
• Connect to rational and logical positions. • The leader seeks benefit to the organization, benefit to the employees, or both.	• Connect to individual goals or values. • By connecting the goal, message, or project to the individual, the leader promotes feelings of well-being, service, and sense of belonging.	• Involve collaboration, consultation, and alliance. • The leader helps employees work together to accomplish a mutually beneficial goal.

So, how do these three approaches play out in the workplace? A leader making a logical appeal—involving the head—might create specific job descriptions and levels so as to standardize hiring and promotional practices. A leader making an emotional appeal—involving the heart—might share with their team their vision, goals, and values around a particular project and ask the team to share theirs so as to connect with the team and build team cohesion. And a leader making a cooperative appeal—involving the hands—might consult with members of a team to understand what's working well and what they're struggling with so as to support greater cooperation and teamwork.

It's important for leaders to have skills in each of these influence strategies because different circumstances will require different approaches. A leader needs to listen to and understand people's unique goals and motivators. They need to have enough experience to know what has worked before—and what has failed. And they need to know who the stakeholders are, as well as the level of influence of those stakeholders. Effective influencers become agents of change by truly listening to all voices and determining the best path forward.

AUTHORITY RELATIONSHIP TYPES

Similar to how we discussed different parenting styles, we're now going to consider the three most common ways people engage with authority, as proposed by William Kahn and Kathy Kram: dependently, counter-dependently, and interdependently.[24]

Dependent: Those with a dependent orientation toward authority see the leader or mentor as superior, valued, and sought after. They tend to conform to match what the leader needs, wants, and values. They often deauthorize themselves and overauthorize leaders. They often suppress their real thoughts and feelings, struggle to generate ideas, and question their decision-making. (As you might have guessed, many who struggle with impostor syndrome engage with authority in this manner.)

Counter-dependent: Those with a counter-dependent orientation toward authority minimize, undermine, or devalue authority. They may dismiss or undermine a supervisor and refuse to cooperate. They may have poor conflict-resolution skills, and so engage in a passive-aggressive process when they feel resistance toward their supervisor. (This type often is at work within those prone to self-sabotage.)

Interdependent: Those with an interdependent orientation toward authority can simultaneously tolerate a hierarchical relationship while also maintaining independence from that authority. They assume that people can make valuable contributions at all levels and in the context of their role, and so are both open to the leader's contribution and confident of their own capacity to contribute. As a result, their role and experience within the hierarchy does not diminish their perception of themselves, how they perform the role, or how they set boundaries. To them, people occupy different roles at different times—but no roles completely define a person, nor do they erase individual power. They do not shy away from sharing their own voice, but also want to hear others' voices; they can collaborate well even with those with different perspectives. (You likely can tell that this is the ideal orientation toward authority for those working to overcome impostor syndrome.)

Moving toward an interdependent model of authority calls for:

- Recognizing the value in this style of authority dynamic (in other words, seeing how it works better for you than the other styles do).
- Choosing environments where you feel both safe and supported in your authorization.
- Respecting the roles/titles of the people around you—and respecting the people in those roles.

- Functioning from a place of self-value, even when you feel threatened or triggered—at which times you know to calmly view the landscape to assess whether any constructive action is needed.
- Regularly seeking feedback from those you trust.
- Engaging in deep self-awareness practices (therapy, meditation).

EXERCISE 6.4: IDENTIFYING YOUR ORIENTATION TOWARD AUTHORITY

Take a moment now to consider whether your typical strategy for dealing with authority has been dependent, counter-dependent, or interdependent. What have been the consequences to you of using this style? Can you describe what your functioning in an interdependent style would look like? What would it take for you to try on a more interdependent style? How might you operationalize the change?

_____

_____

_____

_____

FIVE ARCHETYPES OF TOXIC LEADERS

The subject of toxic leadership is so large it could be its own book. For our purposes here, we've seen in our work that the following five archetypes of toxic leaders are particularly triggering to those struggling with impostor syndrome. You might notice that many toxic leaders exhibit the signs of struggling with impostor syndrome themselves.

TOXIC BOSSES FOR THOSE WITH IMPOSTOR SYNDROME

 PERFECTIONISTIC BOSS "I saw a mistake in that slide." *(Even when the presentation went well)*

 **INSECURE BOSS** "You embarrassed me in that meeting. Next time, I want to be involved in every step."

 **ERRATIC BOSS** One minute "you are a star." The next minute "you are a disappointment."

 **PROVE IT TO ME BOSS** "I am not sure you can handle this project. You are going to have to show me that you can manage it." *(Even though you have done well with similar things in the past)*

  **WITHHOLDING BOSS** "It went okay" or no feedback at all. *(After a successful project)*

Perfectionistic bosses set up unachievable standards. Because of their exacting standards they are oftentimes highly regarded—but they'll always be caught up with what you're *not* doing to the highest standard. Since they focus on the mistakes, they rarely give positive feedback. And though they could see mistakes as an opportunity for growth, they instead see mistakes as a personal flaw or as demonstration of definitive incapability.

YOUR UNSTOPPABLE GREATNESS

Since those with impostor syndrome have a tendency toward people-pleasing and perfectionism, it can be tempting to work for such a boss out of the hope of getting it right. But, unfortunately these bosses can be so overfunctioning, overworking, and detail-oriented that it's hard to ever please them—and so they can be very unhealthy for us. In fact, their perfectionism often leaves them very unsatisfied with their life, and so to work for them can amount to simply sharing in their misery.

Insecure bosses feel very uncomfortable in their position. They exhibit a lot of anxiety about work; they constantly feel under threat, which can make them paranoid. As a result, they tend to micromanage because they see your work as a direct reflection on them and are afraid you'll put them at risk. And even if you consistently produce excellent work, they can struggle to trust you because they are so focused on their internal struggles. One initial appeal of insecure bosses is that they can seem down to earth and/or vulnerable, and it can be tempting to be their Superperson to save them. But, since they're so focused on themselves, they likely won't make you feel that they value your contribution.

Erratic bosses are hard to predict and hard to please. One day, you're the "star" and they're singing your praises; the next day you're the "problem child" and they're flying off the handle. So the people-pleasing tendencies of those of us with impostor syndrome can get us caught in a cycle of trying be on their good side—but that good side is completely out of our hands. In essence, they don't know how to regulate their emotions. The resulting lack of predictability can be very triggering, leading us to spend a lot of time trying to understand how to avoid upsetting them.

"Prove it to me" bosses need to be continually impressed with your current work. There's no resting on your laurels with them; if you do well, you'll get momentary praise, but on the next project they'll act as if they have no trust in your ability—regardless of your track record. That you constantly have to prove yourself is a significant trigger of impostor syndrome because you can feel they really know you—and know that you're not good enough—leaving you desperate to never let them see that you're a fraud.

Withholding bosses are extremely hard to please. They won't give you positive feedback unless you blow them away—which can seem difficult if not impossible to achieve, regardless of the quality of your work. They can be aloof and distant. Constantly struggling to please such a boss is exhausting and terrifying; and as a result of their withholding nature, the minimal feedback you get from them hampers your ability to grow—not only in the organization, but also in your profession.

Many of these leadership types can create competitive dynamics on their teams, which can lead to behaviors that are problematic for those working to overcome impostor syndrome, such as working on your own and not trusting others—whereas ideally we'd strive to get comfortable having a team around us and learn to collaborate well. So, the problematic effects of the boss ripple out to the team and environment as well.

EXERCISE 6.5: IDENTIFYING TOXIC LEADERS

Check which toxic boss behaviors you've experienced.

Perfectionist

❑ They're exacting and hard to please.

❑ They overfunction and overwork.

❑ They're obsessed with mistakes.

Insecure

❑ They're anxious about their position.

❑ They constantly worry about *your* performance.

❑ They micromanage.

Erratic

❑ They're unpredictable.

❑ They're hard to please.

❑ They're emotionally dysregulated or unstable.

"Prove It to Me"

❑ Their appreciation of your work is fleeting.

❑ They make you feel compelled to constantly prove yourself.

❑ They make you feel they see through you—and aren't impressed.

Withholding

❑ They rarely give positive feedback.

❑ They rarely give constructive, growth-based feedback in general.

❑ They can be aloof and distant.

Note that these different archetypes of toxic bosses aren't singular; any one boss can have aspects of more than one type. What's important is that you learn to identify the characteristics that can be problematic for you. We especially hope to help you identify problematic behaviors even with brief exposure—such as when you're interviewing for a new role. The interview questions in the following sidebar are designed to help you assess a boss's style—and whether that style would be healthy or unhealthy for you.

INTERVIEW QUESTIONS FOR DETECTING TOXIC BOSSES

In your next job interview, the answers you get from asking some or all of the following questions could help you assess if working for that boss would be a dream or a nightmare.

Question: What are the characteristics of people who succeed here?

Be on the alert for unhealthy work characteristics codes, such as "Working until the job is done" (read: workaholic) or "Those with type A personalities" (read: perfectionistic). You want to hear mention of skill-based qualities relevant to your profession—plus that a wide variety of types of people are successful there.

Question: How would you describe your leadership style?

You're looking for references to focusing on supporting the development of the individuals and the team.

Question: How do you respond when a worker makes a mistake?

You're looking for a "growth mindset"—where mistakes are (1) seen as normal and human, and (2) are seen as an opportunity for learning.

Question: How does work-life balance get supported on your team?

You'll want to hear a distinct concern about the importance of setting healthy boundaries. You'll want to know that self-care is valued; in the best-case scenario, the organization offers very concrete benefits focused on employee well-being.

Question: How are growth and professional advancement supported here?

You want to hear concrete opportunities for you to grow, such as training, learning and development opportunities, performance review processes that lead to concrete pathways for promotion, and clear and explicit delineation of roles so that it's evident what skills are required for obtaining the next level.

PERFORMANCE REVIEW PROCESSES

Another important piece to consider when dealing with toxic bosses is their evaluation of your performance. As it happens, a toxic boss is likely to be an incredibly poor evaluator of performance. (We'll return to that point lower down.) The trouble is, those of us who struggle with impostor syndrome often find it difficult to positively evaluate our own performance—which can affect our advancement and compensation. So it's important to develop really solid habits around evaluating your performance. To follow are several behaviors related to self-review that are common for those with impostor syndrome—as well as what we'll want to do instead.

MANY WITH IMPOSTOR SYNDROME …	WHAT YOU WANT TO DO INSTEAD
Avoid working on your self-review because it makes you anxious.	Create a document where you will record your wins and value add (with quantifiable evidence and examples) throughout the year.
Provide minimal descriptions of your contributions.	Develop complex, detailed descriptions of the work you've done.
Underestimate your performance.	Request support from mentors and trusted others in accurately assessing your performance.
Focus on your developmental issues and struggles more than anything else.	Address any developmental issues or struggles you may have, but don't overestimate or overfocus on them.
Don't have an ask.	Value yourself enough to consider what ask during the performance review is appropriate (e.g., promotion or timeline around a promotion; bonus; raise; financial support for professional development).

EXERCISE 6.6: YOUR NEW PERFORMANCE REVIEW PROCESSES

With this exercise you put the recommendations in the accompanying table into action. Essentially, we want you to turn that table into a to-do list that you will gradually work on and complete before your next review period. Today, we want you to:

❏ Establish the document where you will catalog your wins and achievements throughout the year.

❏ Create a number of alerts set at periodic intervals that will prompt you to make progress in your review document. It's important that you develop this into a consistent habit.

We said earlier that it's important to develop really solid habits around evaluating your performance because toxic bosses are often very poor at evaluating others' performance. In addition, supervisors are often not trained how to provide solid feedback on performance reviews—and as a result produce an insufficient, rushed assessment viewed through the lens of whatever biases they hold. To follow is chart of some of the types of biases that can affect performance reviews.

Types of Bias That Can Affect Performance Reviews

BIAS	HOW IT'S EXHIBITED
Confirmatory Bias	Rating someone in a manner that confirms existing beliefs while ignoring any contrary information or data.
Shifting Standards	Rating someone where the bar set on specific criteria differs according to the person being rated.
Halo/Horns Effect	Rating is amplified based on prior beliefs. This is essentially confirmation bias on steroids.
Similarity Bias	Rating someone more positively because they are similar to the reviewer in some way that they value.
Primacy Effect	Rating someone based on something that occurred early on in knowing them. (For example, they made a colossal mistake in their first 90 days, and the reviewer won't forget it.)
Recency Effect	Rating someone solely based on just the most recent part of the review period, not the entire period.
Central Tendency Bias	When using performance rating scales, rating most employees in the middle of the scale.
Leniency Bias	Rating someone more favorably than is warranted, without noting the ways they could improve.
Idiosyncratic Rater Bias	Rating others higher for skills the rater is weaker in, and rating others lower for skills the rater is stronger in (or thinks they're stronger in).
Self-Rater Bias	When individuals' rating of themselves reflects more on their self-image or self-esteem than their actual performance.

If you're currently working for a toxic boss, have you already received a performance review from them? If so, then your next step is to consider that review in light of their toxic behavior and limitations, and manage whatever comes up for you in revisiting that review—especially if it's a distorted, inaccurate picture of your performance. We hope that, having reviewed the biases that can distort their assessment, you're able to extract out of their review a representative evaluation of your performance.

If you're a manager or are responsible for someone else's review, it's important to note any bias tendencies that you may have and work toward delivering your performance reviews in a more unbiased way.

WHAT'S YOUR LEADERSHIP STYLE?

There's an additional angle to this discussion. We mentioned earlier that many toxic bosses themselves struggle with impostor syndrome. What if you yourself are a supervisor, boss, mentor, or teacher? If so, you likely display some of the toxic leadership behaviors we've reviewed. Do you see yourself in what you've read here? Maybe take a moment to identify which behaviors you've displayed in your leadership role. Now, can you think about ways you could break the habit of those behaviors? The fact that you're working through this book demonstrates that you're committed to breaking free from your impostor syndrome. We encourage you to stick with it, not just for yourself but also for everyone you work with.

KEY TAKEAWAYS

In closing this chapter, we hope that:

- You've considered which parenting style(s) you were subjected to in your early family, as well as how that/those styles show up in your experience as an adult.
- You've developed an understanding of various authorizing and deauthorizing behaviors—and considered how you might concretely transform any authorizing behaviors that harm you into behaviors that would benefit you.
- You've developed an awareness of the three Head, Heart, and Hands strategies of influence and how they may play out in the workplace.
- You've developed an awareness of the three most common ways people engage with authority; you've considered which orientation you employ; and you've considered how you might move toward an interdependent model, if necessary.
- You've developed an awareness of the different toxic leadership styles and have identified which ones you are vulnerable to.
- You've created a new process around how you deal with performance reviews.

- You're aware of how a toxic boss's behavior can show up in your performance review, and how to ensure you have an accurate counternarrative.
- You recognize that working on your impostor syndrome helps to ensure you don't become a toxic boss or coworker.

Chapter 7

PROTECTING YOUR IDENTITY

By its very nature, impostor syndrome makes us feel like a fraud, like we don't belong, especially in the inner circles of people we admire. It can make us feel we must conform to the environments around us to try and demonstrate that we're capable, that we're good enough. Impostor syndrome can be a definite threat to our identity and sense of self. And if we're from a historically marginalized group—especially when our performance and ability to succeed has been stereotypically tied to that identity, for example if we have a disability, or are a woman, BIPOC, or first-generation, etc.—we likely have already experienced a sense of otherness, a lack of belonging, and the need to prove ourselves just on account of the discriminatory systems and prejudicial thinking and behavior we encounter every day. Unfortunately, impostor syndrome can make us feel on the fringes of the groups that we definitely belong to—such as our work group, and even groups of people with similar identities. This can bring us to hide, diminish, or devalue our identities, perhaps to the point of remaining silent about the discrimination and oppression we regularly experience. We might hide because we fear being perceived as receiving or needing preferential treatment, which additionally triggers the idea that we are less than. But being different does not mean "less than"—even though discriminatory systems can make us feel like that. Difference is just different.

You may have read in the popular press the notion that oppression causes impostor syndrome. It's great click-bait material, but there is no research to date suggesting that impostor syndrome is caused by oppression and discrimination. Rigid roles and family dynamics set the foundation for impostor syndrome, which is why it's experienced by people from privileged groups as well as people from oppressed groups; no one is exempt. Of course, oppressive systems do benefit from and sustain impostor syndrome by triggering it, since someone treated as a diversity hire, for example, might feel forced to work that much harder to prove that they do belong. Unfortunately, systems consciously or unconsciously use impostor syndrome to benefit the bottom line—to the detriment of those who are dismissed and excluded. The following table shares just some of the ways this can occur.

Ways Oppressive Institutions Reinforce and Benefit from Impostor Syndrome

DISCRIMINATORY REINFORCER	IMPOSTOR SYNDROME BEHAVIOR	THEIR BENEFIT
They make you feel you're "less than." They make you feel you may have attained a position only because of your identity (e.g., you're considered a diversity hire).	You overwork to prove yourself.	They get the work product of more than one employee.
They gaslight you when you express that you're experiencing negative treatment based on your identity (e.g., you share that you believe you're being treated unfairly because of an identity factor—and you're told that you're not, that it happens to everyone).	You don't trust your own experience.	Your insecurity and your struggle to trust yourself results in requiring and relying on external validation from others.
You lack the support that others from privileged groups receive or the support you get is insufficient (e.g., you're assigned a mentor who doesn't offer you much—even though they readily offer support to others who are more like themselves).	It reinforces the idea that you must succeed alone, without help—and so you don't build a Dream Team.	It saves them money and resources. Your success costs them less. They are less invested in you.
They make you feel it requires special treatment to get you up to par (e.g., you have to attend special leadership trainings). Or that you require a significant amount of feedback related to your culture or identity (e.g., "you don't have executive presence because you're not loud or demonstrative"; or "you're too demonstrative or too angry").	You feel something is wrong with you.	It builds organizational loyalty to them because you feel like no one else will want you, so you have to stay.
You experience microaggressions in reference to your performance (e.g., if you're an Asian woman and are told you're not assertive enough in negotiations).	This reinforces the idea that you're not good enough and you don't belong.	It makes you hyperfocus on never standing out for any negative reason, especially regarding making mistakes.

What's important to see is that these environments may not have directly originated your impostor syndrome, but they most certainly trigger it—and they know how to sustain it, benefit from it, and use it to advance their agenda. So, if you're from a privileged group and are committed to eradicating impostor syndrome in the organizations and systems you belong to, it's vital that you commit to diversity, equity, and inclusion efforts supporting the appreciation and valuing of differences and fair treatment for all. Healthy environments benefit everyone.

And if you're from a historically marginalized group, before you commit to work for an organization it's vital to examine its commitment to diversity, equity, and inclusion—both in words and in action. But how can you tell if an organization will support you and your individual differences? Just words are not enough. Beautifully crafted DEI statements and committees are just facades if there are no actions to support them: actions like having a significant percentage of diverse employees, especially in positions of power. Another essential indication is how the organization or system addresses complaints made against it, and if they respond by implementing institutional change—or just focus on exonerating themselves. Of course, if you're considering joining an organization, you won't necessarily have access to the whole story. But you could make a practice of researching the companies in your industry that you may wish to join at some point, and follow all mentions of them in the news. You could also explore the pages of websites like Glassdoor to learn what employees have to say. Look out for references to leaders being defensive or dismissive.

But let's say you're wondering if the place where you currently work deserves your continued contribution. If an investigation revealed that managers needed better training in handling particular issues (such as microaggressions in the workplace), you'd want to see that they engage that process with expediency and urgency. You also want to see managers speaking competently and openly about issues of diversity, equity, and inclusion; being receptive to feedback; and facilitating constructive changes. In inclusive environments, employees feel welcomed, supported, and heard. In equitable environments, everyone feels they're treated fairly. In diverse environments, there is room for all kinds of identities—room for people with all kinds of ways of succeeding, expressing themselves, and just being. Developing these types of healthy organizations takes consistent work, intention, and commitment. An organization that is fully committed to DEI knows that there is no end point; they can never declare they have reached an "anti-racist or DEI state." It is an ongoing process.

Part of that process includes addressing triggers of impostor syndrome in members of historically marginalized groups, such as actions that reinforce otherness, as mentioned in the accompanying sidebar.

YOUR UNSTOPPABLE GREATNESS

ADDITIONAL TRIGGERS OF IMPOSTOR SYNDROME FOR HISTORICALLY MARGINALIZED PEOPLE

Discrimination: Discrimination involves provocative or patronizing behaviors intended to diminish another, such as harassment or unfavorable treatment.

Microaggression: Microaggressions are statements, actions, or incidents of indirect, subtle, or unintentional discrimination, like speaking over someone in a meeting or employing stereotypical descriptions.

Isolation: When isolation is in play a member of a historically marginalized group is one of very few and feels no sense of community.

Lack of mentorship or sponsorship: You either have a formal mentor who is disengaged, or you don't have a sponsor advocating for you and your advancement.

Inequitable treatment or access: You see yourself being treated differently and not receiving the same benefits or access to certain resources or opportunities (e.g., like others get the benefit of the doubt on their work or competence, even if their work is subpar).

Gaslighting: You're experiencing bias or incidents related to your identity—but when you share it, people are quick to minimize it and diminish it as having nothing to do with identity, often suggesting that it didn't happen, or that it happens to everyone.

THE DOUBLE IMPACT OF IMPOSTOR SYNDROME

Unfortunately, the above types of external triggers exacerbate the established internal thoughts and feelings that come with impostor syndrome. We call this the "double impact" of impostor syndrome.

DOUBLE IMPACT OF IMPOSTOR SYNDROME

INTERNAL THOUGHTS OF IMPOSTOR SYNDROME

"I need to prove myself."
"Do I deserve to be here?"
"Everyone is better than me."

EXTERNAL COMMUNICATIONS

"Are you really a culture fit?"
"You are a diversity hire."
"I am not sure you are good enough."

As you can imagine, the double impact of impostor syndrome makes it even harder for historically marginalized people to overcome their oppressive experience. Fortunately, research has indicated that one of the most powerful interventions is feeling part of a community of like members.[25] For example, if you feel your impostor syndrome is being reinforced because you're Black, then you'll want to work to build community with other Black people, both at your level and at a senior level. This adds another layer to consider when you're building the Dream Team: your sense(s) of identity needs to be a significant consideration. This is because that community can serve as a witness of your experience and can provide the validation that what you're seeing and experiencing is real—and has likely been felt by them as well. Further, they can provide you with strategy, ideas, and support when you feel isolated, alone, and "less than." We've said this before but it's worth emphasizing: one of the greatest factors in sustaining impostor syndrome is isolation. When we've been in the throes of impostor syndrome, we've often suffered alone sheerly out of fearing that revealing our struggles to someone else could lead to being exposed as a fraud. Fear is an automatic negative thought (ANT) that serves to reinforce a component of impostor syndrome. Countering that ANT becomes extremely critical as you battle impostor syndrome. When you struggle with impostor syndrome and you're from a historically marginalized community, the mantra should be FORWARD TOGETHER, NEVER ALONE. Choosing a healthy community is crucially important, especially since you're learning about toxic leaders and systems. The health of your community will always matter and your ability to choose members of that community will hopefully become much more honed as you work through this book. Through this book, we are teaching you to stay away from toxic behaviors, leaders, and systems, and to move toward healthier, communal, and more self-aware people, who will be essential to your growth and maintaining your healthy boundaries and distance from impostor syndrome.

OTHER CONSEQUENCES FOR MARGINALIZED GROUPS

We've mentioned that research indicates there is a correlation between impostor syndrome and anxiety, depression, burnout, and decreased self-esteem. Unfortunately, the list of potential negative effects gets even longer for those from marginalized groups. To follow we discuss some of the research findings for different historically marginalized groups; as you review them, consider if and how they affect you.

RACIAL GROUPS IMPACTS

The term "minority-status stress" refers to the stress of being a member of a minority community. Minority-status stress has long been strongly correlated with psychological stress in research literature.[26] In a groundbreaking study in 2013, Dr. Kevin Cokley and others demonstrated that, for Latinx, African Americans, and Asian Americans, the feelings of impostor syndrome were a stronger predictor of mental health and psychological distress than were the stressors related to being a minority.[27] This study further emphasizes the importance of people of color working on impostor syndrome; these additional factors are too detrimental to be ignored.

Several studies have shown that for Black people, impostor syndrome is highly correlated with depression, survivor's guilt, lower grade point average, low self-esteem, and high psychological distress.[28] Another study in 2017 found that Black people with impostor syndrome are likely to experience greater feelings of depression brought on by experiences of discrimination. It was also shown that perceived discrimination and impostor feelings were a strong predictor of anxiety. Impostor syndrome can affect performance at school, sense of self, and how one copes with distress, and can worsen the experience of discrimination. It can also create a greater sense of survivor's guilt—which means that, as you succeed in moving away from toxic behavior, you may feel bad about the people you're leaving behind.[29]

CASE STUDY: SHARICE

A Black woman in her forties, Sharice had made a significant name for herself in the nonprofit arts world. She was charged with building from the ground up a program focused on giving grants to artists doing important cultural and political work all over the world. The job was her dream role—but she felt she didn't deserve it given how many talented people work in the creative space. As a result, she overworked and overfunctioned to prove that she belonged and to demonstrate that the organization could trust her. However, at every turn, the organization put up barriers. They made her explain why she did what she did even though they had granted her the authority to do it. They reduced her funding. They pretended to give her free rein, and then added people to her team without her consent—people who (no surprise) created chaos and sabotaged her efforts. And though the organization as a whole considered itself liberal and socially conscious, many employees engaged in racial microaggressions. After a few years, Sharice was exhausted and burned out from fighting so many battles, and disappointed at how much her progress had been hindered. She felt defeated and wanted to move on, but she was plagued by guilt at the thought of leaving her team behind—many of whom she'd mentored for years, watching them grow. She knew there was a good chance that the program she ran would collapse if she left. She also got a lot of pressure from colleagues, mentors, family, and friends to persevere given the importance of her goal, but she was struggling under the huge cost to herself.

Survivor's guilt is keeping Sharice stuck. She is torn about what to do despite her sheer exhaustion, which is exacerbated by the sadness and depletion resulting from the constant microaggressions she receives. While she does have a community around her, her community members don't realize that their recommendations reinforce the self-sacrificial and burnout behavior that fuels her impostor syndrome. She needs to add to her Dream Team a big-picture person and an action planner to help her figure out what to do next.

It's interesting to note that the research suggests that different populations may experience impostor syndrome differently, which could call for unique interventions. Two studies headed by Dr. Kevin Cokley found that Asian Americans actually experienced greater impostor feelings than do Black and Latinx students. It was hypothesized that this may be true because of the "model minority stereotype"—such as high academic achievement—that Asian Americans are often held to.[30] Annabelle L. Atkin and fellow researchers have found that Asian Americans who internalized the model minority stereotype were more likely to feel pressure to live up to expectations of being "successful, intelligent, and hardworking."[31] Of course, these are some of the key concepts that foster impostor syndrome. A more recent study headed by Meifen Wei found a strong correlation between impostor feelings and psychological distress, particularly around issues of shame, such as others viewing them negatively, or dishonoring their family due to perceived deficits.[32] So, if you're Asian and dealing with impostor syndrome, it will be critical to fight the model minority stereotype and learn to define success for yourself, outside the rigid norms set by others.

That same study by Meifen Wei and others found that self-compassion can be an effective intervention to mediate the experience of shame. For more, see the Self-Compassion sidebar.

SELF-COMPASSION

We can practice self-compassion by being understanding and kind to ourselves when we suffer, fail, or feel inadequate. Kristin Neff describes the three elements of self-compassion as:

- Self-kindness versus self-judgment,
- Common humanity versus isolation, and
- Mindfulness versus overidentification (getting "caught up and swept away by negative" thoughts and feelings).

When you struggle with impostor syndrome, showing yourself self-compassion can mean:

- Being conscious of and kind about the words you use to talk about yourself.
- Prioritizing and maintaining healthy self-care practices.
- Internalizing your cheerleaders and ignoring your harsh critics.
- Acknowledging that treating yourself with kindness will advance your goals more than self-criticism ever will.
- Building community and allowing yourself to be vulnerable in it.

For more, check out self-compassion.org and Dr. Neff's books on the subject, *Self-Compassion* and *Fierce Self-Compassion*.

FIRST-GENERATION IMPACTS

Navigating new experiences can be triggering to all of us who struggle with impostor syndrome. But imagine navigating a new experience that no one you know has ever experienced. Research has shown that the stress felt by first-generation students (those who are the first in their family to enroll in higher education, enter a particular field, or hold a particular role) may be more acute when they experience impostor syndrome[33]—which can lead to further isolation and entrenchment of impostor feelings, every incident of struggle standing as further proof that you don't belong and you won't make it. Indeed, it has been found that in competitive environments impostor feelings are strong predictors of class engagement, attendance, dropout rates, and grades.[34]

If the above describes your situation, it's important to understand that there is a learning curve for every new venture we set out on. We need to give ourselves time to learn the culture and the expectations and to build the community that can help us navigate these new systems. Practice self-compassion, and take pride in the courage of your goals.

GENDER IMPACTS

References to impostor syndrome in the popular press and on social media can make it seem as though it's predominantly women who experience it—but this take is not supported in the research literature. It's likely that this mythology got started because Pauline Rose Clance and Suzanne Ament Imes initially studied impostor syndrome with women in the late 1970s and early 1980s. In a 2016 *Slate* article, Clance stated that "women are more likely to say some of their doubts and fears, and there's more pressure on men not to do so."[35]

However, the impacts of impostor syndrome are experienced differently. For example, women have been shown to report impostor beliefs more often than men do, and have "higher scores"—meaning that their frequency of experiencing it may be higher.[36] This seems not unexpected given that research has often found that women are more likely to face their fears when they experience impostor syndrome—which would inevitably increase the frequency of impostor feelings.[37] A 2017 examination of gender roles found that study participants who identified as "masculine" or "androgynous" scored lower on impostor syndrome than did those who identified as "feminine."[38] This interesting finding may show a correlation between traditional gender roles and impostor feelings—which is all the more reason to challenge traditional, especially female, gender roles. In addition, another study headed by Kevin Cokley found that gender-stigma consciousness (the extent to which an individual is chronically aware of his/her/their gender's stigmatized status—in other words, being also judged by your gender rather than by your performance alone) was a significant predictor of impostor syndrome for both women and men, but stronger for women. They also found that impostor syndrome was a significant predictor of higher GPA for women but not for men. This is consistent with other research showing that women with impostor syndrome work harder and are more engaged in school activities, which often leads to higher grades.[39]

Studies have shown that men experiencing impostor syndrome can lead to them underperforming, avoiding goals and feedback, and engaging with less-competent peers.[40] Men can focus their concern on mastery of particular skills, which causes them to avoid taking risks and remain in roles, positions, and environments that they don't enjoy, leading to career stagnation.

It's our hope that the research literature on impostor syndrome continues to explore the different facets of the phenomenon, especially related to how different populations experience it, including gender nonbinary individuals. Data-backed understanding of the real impacts of impostor syndrome can help us to find better interventions so more can overcome it.

SOME NEGATIVE IMPACTS OF IMPOSTOR SYNDROME

Those struggling with impostor syndrome can feel:

- depressed
- anxious
- like a failure/loser
- like a fraud/impostor
- less than/flawed
- never good enough
- unqualified/ underqualified/ insufficient
- pathetic

- stupid
- useless
- ashamed
- unworthy
- constantly judged and scrutinized
- like an alien/other/ square peg
- alone/lonely/ unsupported/isolated

- ostracized
- frustrated/angry
- insecure
- diminished
- denied
- invisible
- patronized/infantilized/ condescended to
- stereotyped

EXERCISE 7.1: INTERSECTING EFFECTS OF IMPOSTOR SYNDROME

We all have more than one identity—race, gender, ethnicity, etc.—and our intersecting identities likely affect our experience of impostor syndrome. Take a moment to go back to the sections earlier in this chapter that highlight how the specific aspects of your identity may be particularly impacted by impostor syndrome. In the information you find there, identify what you've experienced (say, discrimination-related depression, or shame). (See also the accompanying Some Negative Impacts of Impostor Syndrome sidebar.) Then, consider how you can support yourself in attending to these effects of your impostor syndrome.

IDENTITY	IMPACT	POSSIBLE INTERVENTION

In this chapter, we have taken you through how your impostor syndrome is affected very directly by your identity. We hope you've become more aware of how discrimination, micro-aggressions, and bias affect your impostor syndrome, and how it can impact your success. However, we hope you also feel empowered to understand that there are a variety of interventions that are incredibly powerful to reducing your impostor syndrome in your individual experience.

KEY TAKEAWAYS

In closing this chapter, we hope that:

- You're aware of the ways oppressive institutions reinforce and benefit from impostor syndrome.
- You're aware of the unique impacts and additional triggers for historically marginalized groups—part of the double impact of impostor syndrome.
- You've considered the various ways impostor syndrome affects the different aspects of your identity.
- You understand that eradicating impostor syndrome everywhere calls for committing to diversity, equity, and inclusion.

PART THREE
ACTUALIZATION

Chapter 8

BELONGING IN HEALTHY SYSTEMS

Many who struggle with impostor syndrome are very familiar with being alone and succeeding on our own. That's often our preference, since we can distrust people out of fear they'll harm us or betray us. But belonging is a critical aspect of healing and recovering from impostor syndrome, so we must actively work on learning how to connect and build community.

When we screened students for our Own Your Greatness Master Class, one of the most common fears we uncovered concerned the group setting of the class. Some asked, "How will I know my confidentiality is protected?" And, "What if I don't want to share during a particular week?" Or, "How will you determine who is in what group?" When we listen to these fears, we heard in them the pain of the past, the familiarity with isolation, and the desperate desire to heal in secrecy. Most students in the master class enter with extreme cautiousness and hesitancy. It often takes a while before the first student takes a risk and models that for the others. This is essential since the greater vulnerability the students can express about their experience and process, the greater their outcome will be. As it happens, by the end of the three-month master class almost all the students report that what they'll miss the most is the time they spent with their fellow members; and how seeing their classmates take risks, share, struggle, use their skills, and have wins was incredibly inspiring and encouraged them to do the same. They are learning in vivo one of the most critical skills of recovery from impostor syndrome: the strength of belonging to a healthy system—something some of them were experiencing for the first time.

We've discussed how an unhealthy family system—the first place where we learn about belonging—lays a fertile ground for impostor syndrome. So, it's no surprise that, if your first system created fear or anxiety for you, you'd be suspicious of other groups and reluctant to trust belonging to any system. But, as we've shared, your ability to overcome your impostor syndrome and to sustain the gains you made is dependent upon working on issues of belonging and, eventually, finding a safe place in healthy groups.

CASE STUDY: LISA (continued from page 72)

When Lisa was in her postdoctoral training right before the job mentioned in our TEDx talk—when she was still in the throes of impostor syndrome—her supervisor remarked insightfully that she noticed Lisa tended to exist on the periphery of groups, that she'd put in a toe but wouldn't make much more commitment than that. Lisa had never seen that in herself, but once she reflected on how she engaged with groups, either academic or professional, the insight really resonated for her. She was very good at looking like she was fully committed—by speaking up in groups, taking leadership roles, and being congenial—but she had very clear internal walls. In other words, even though she looked emotionally available and present, she kept an emotional distance, and didn't socialize with those from school or work. When her supervisor shared this insight, Lisa viscerally feared she was going to encourage her to change these habits, and that frightened her. Lisa immediately thought: "What groups do I want to belong to? Do I trust or even like the people in the groups I'm connected to? What would being more committed to these groups even look like?" These are often the fears we struggle with as we work on the skills of belonging, connection, and being vulnerable with others.

How do we learn to repair those experiences of belonging and to build a sense of trust and connection in groups? The first piece of that calls for reflecting on some of those early experiences of groups and how we managed to cope or even just survive within them. For many of us, we kept ourselves safe and protected by remaining at the periphery of a group. The periphery experience can have different dimensions, including looking like you're engaging and committed but, in truth, no one really knows you or has access to other parts of you. Many of us orchestrate the kind of experience that we want others to have with us—and can get uncomfortable if they veer away from that. For example, we can be very oriented toward people-pleasing and want others to like us—so, if they don't like us, we can find it troubling, hyperfocus on it, and want to change their experience of us. Another approach involves attempting to control the group, either through leadership or influence, to ensure the group behaves the way we're used to. But aside from trying to lead in particular ways, true "follow-ership" or collaboration can be very difficult for us because we're not in control, and we know we'll have to trust others in the process.

EXERCISE 8.1: REFLECTING ON PERIPHERIES

Do you strive to remain on the periphery of groups? Take a moment to reflect on the ways you do that, like not identifying with the group, or not allowing yourself to be vulnerable with anyone.

_____

_____

_____

PSYCHOLOGICAL SAFETY

One task to work on is our definition and expectation of safety. "Safety" can't mean that we're absolutely protected from any negative experience, so we'll want to look for psychological safety *within* these groups and communities we're practicing belonging in. "Psychological safety" is a concept that was coined in 1999 by Harvard Business School professor and organizational behavioral scientist Amy Edmondson. "Psychological safety" means feeling safe from negative consequences or reprisals for speaking up, sharing ideas, conveying concerns, or making mistakes. In order to create psychological safety, an organization, system, group, or community must be able to:

- Encourage everyone to be honest, truthful, open, and empathetic in communication.
- Have a growth mindset regarding failure by supporting experimentation and risk-taking and embracing mistakes as a time for everyone to learn and grow.
- Support healthy engagement in conflict and disagreement, seeing conflict as the potential for discussion, collaboration, conversation, dialectic (investigation of opinions), and debate.
- Create space for new, creative, or innovative ideas.
- Engage in feedback in a constructive method focused on development and growth.
- Treat members with respect and acceptance—no stars or scapegoats!—focusing on everyone's strengths, skills, and competencies.

- Ensure that team structure and roles are clear and that there is cohesion among members.[41]

Your goal when working on belonging to a group, organization, or community is to feel that most if not all of these criteria are met. And when they are, everyone benefits. Studies have shown that organizations that promote psychological safety tend to have greater employee engagement, and their employees learn more from mistakes and are more innovative.[42] When we seek out communities that don't reinforce unhealthy ideals, behaviors, and culture, we're better able to work through our impostor syndrome.

LEADERSHIP STYLES AND THEIR IMPACT ON PSYCHOLOGICAL SAFETY

A study by McKinsey & Company found two leadership styles were particularly effective in creating a sense of psychological safety:

Consultative leaders maintain two-way communication with team members by requesting input and welcoming suggestions; they then make decisions based on that input.

Supportive leaders build trust, encourage teamwork, help teams overcome challenges, and address relational dynamics.

In addition, both leadership styles foster coworkers supporting each other.[43]

Somewhat ironically, we might not be comfortable with some of these aspects of psychological safety, like open communication, consistent feedback, having no identified "star" members, or environments that practice conflict management in a way that resolves it productively and constructively.[44] Our impostor syndrome may tell us that we're better off avoiding conflict or hiding our feelings, or that we need (to strive) to be a star in organizations—especially if we don't know how to do otherwise. Well, we want to do otherwise because cultural norms that reinforce psychological safety are healthy for us and help us to lean toward group affiliation. Our ability to belong and connect while combating our impostor syndrome depends on these experiences of psychological safety.

EXERCISE 8.2: ASSESSING PSYCHOLOGICAL SAFETY

Being able to assess a group's psychological safety becomes incredibly important as you determine whether you will commit to these groups. So let's create an opportunity to practice your psychological safety observational skills. For each of these qualities, explore the questions openly. It might be helpful to use a group that you're currently on the fringes of but are considering becoming more involved in.

PSYCHOLOGICAL SAFETY QUALITY	EXPLORATION QUESTIONS	THE ASSESSMENT OF YOUR GROUP
Honesty and openness	Do I see people being forthright with each other? Do I experience very little to no gossiping? Do people engage in good listening skills?	
Growth mindset	Are mistake-making and risk-taking valued? Do I see people at all levels in the group publicly making and sharing their mistakes? Does the group engage in a process of learning from mistakes? Do they *not* engage in blaming, valuing perfectionism, and beliefs that people's capacity is fixed?	
Healthy conflict	Is conflict and disagreement embraced in a collaborative way? Do the outcomes of the conflict reflect new ways of thinking or doing? Does the conflict seem nonadversarial? Do they *refuse* to engage in ganging up on each other, passive aggressiveness, and always having a winner?	
Creative ideas	Am I allowed to share new ideas even if they go against the current way of doing things? Does everyone in the group or organization have the equal ability to share ideas? Do people respond to ideas with support rather than dismissing or disproving them?	

PSYCHOLOGICAL SAFETY QUALITY	EXPLORATION QUESTIONS	THE ASSESSMENT OF YOUR GROUP
Constructive feedback	Is feedback given regularly and fairly immediately? Does the feedback include behavioral examples with ideas of how to remedy it? Are people allowed to change (i.e., it is expected that they will grow and change and not be stuck in a role other people choose for them)? Is feedback allowed to go in every direction (i.e., everyone can provide feedback to each other)?	
Respect and acceptance	Are differences honored, appreciated, and respected? Are everyone's strengths seen, valued, and utilized? Do I feel accepted?	
Team structure and cohesion	Does the group feel cohesive and connected, and yet also not engaging in groupthink (i.e., that everyone has to think and behave the same)? Does everyone understand their role and the responsibilities that come with it? Where responsibility overlaps, is any resulting concern handled openly and honestly?	

• • •

Learning to examine the safety of an organization is a very important tool. It helps us to assess with more than just instinct and gut—which can be misleading, especially if we have trauma around systems—and to move toward concrete methods of assessing where there is safety and where it is lacking. Now, we will caution you here: beware of any perfectionistic tendencies you may have. As you examine groups and organizations, don't write them off if they come up lacking. Instead, take the opportunity to identify the places where the organization is trying and perhaps succeeding, and then consider how you can improve the psychological safety of the areas where they're not hitting the mark. Try to at least attempt getting what you need to feel safe. This opportunity also challenges your skills around communicating difficult things, getting your needs met, tolerating discomfort, and embracing your agency—all of which are part of contending with your impostor syndrome. That said, if you make attempts to get your needs met around psychological safety, but are hindered from making progress, then it would probably make sense to not commit to *these* organizations. In which case, we encourage you to keep looking!

PERFECTIONISM AND HEALTHY BELONGING

When we think about perfectionism and impostor syndrome, we often think about how our perfectionism affects our evaluation of ourselves. But perfectionism can show up in our evaluation of others as well, and it can be a significant reason why we self-marginalize in group settings. When we're working on belonging we need to learn to give up interpersonal perfectionism or "other-oriented" perfectionism—meaning, not holding up others to our sense of "perfect." This is because when we engage in other-oriented perfectionism in our evaluation of people we can get caught up in:

- Being judgmental of others and their very human behaviors.
- Having such rigid and unrealistically high expectations that others are unlikely to meet them—and end up disappointing us.
- Not communicating our expectations because we believe they are universal standards.
- Not offering feedback because we believe others are unchangeable.
- Being unforgiving or unfairly harsh when someone makes a mistake.

In *Own Your Greatness* we focused on letting go of self-oriented perfectionism; here we want to challenge any other-oriented perfectionism that may be getting in our way. Interpersonal perfectionism creates a level of rigidity that can diminish the quality of our relationships and prevent us from truly connecting with others. Combating other-oriented perfectionism can mean:

- Having empathy and tolerance for others.
- Appreciating that everyone's expectations and standards are different, and clearly communicating our own.
- Constructively addressing disappointments and disconnects.
- Learning to truly forgive and build with people after a rupture.
- Accepting that all relationships have flaws and will run into issues—and they need to develop and mature through disagreement and positive conflict.

VULNERABILITY

Practicing these healthier interpersonal behaviors can really alter the dynamic of remaining at the periphery and feeling we must go it alone. But as we battle with interpersonal perfectionism we also have to work on our vulnerability. When struggling with impostor syndrome we usually try to prevent ourselves from feeling vulnerable for fear of exposing our flaws, faults, and mistakes—the ultimate revelation of our fraudulence. But now that we know we are *not* frauds, "vulnerability" can connote letting others in, showing our true selves, allowing ourselves to be human and whole. Practicing vulnerability will require conscious effort since it's not our natural state or preference. We must practice vulnerability with the intention of creating better experiences of community for ourselves. This calls for really being aware of how we keep ourselves walled up, hide mistakes, and prevent ourselves from being known in ways we consider unflattering or embarrassing. We must take a very conscious audit of the ways we hide our true human selves.

EXERCISE 8.3: AUDITING VULNERABILITY

Take a moment to consider and describe some of the behaviors you engage in that protect you from being vulnerable in interpersonal settings. For example: not taking on roles or responsibilities that might show you lack skills in an area, being closed off about certain parts of yourself, not admitting to missteps, etc.

_____

_____

_____

_____

This is not to say we encourage you to immediately risk being completely vulnerable. Nor are we suggesting you lean too much on friends, family, or colleagues, hoping they'll "fix" things for you. You'll want to give yourself time to adjust to the process and proceed in ever-increasing increments as others demonstrate they can be trustworthy (in a nonperfectionistic and human way). Vulnerability involves sharing things that feel appropriate to the context—sharing a bit of your humanity and whole self.

RELATIONAL RESILIENCE

Impostor syndrome can make us "bruise prone," meaning that when something injurious, embarrassing, or revealing happens, the resulting bruise can feel overwhelming—and so we're desperate to avoid that pain. And so recovering from impostor syndrome calls for developing relational resilience: the capacity to spring back and recover quickly from interpersonal difficulties—to be less bruise prone. Resilience requires the ability to adaptively process and cope with difficulties; it requires pliability, flexibility, communication and problem-solving skills, the ability to manage strong emotions, and confidence in your competencies. Learning to recover and be resilient in the face of interpersonal difficulties are skills we need to consistently work on as part of the process of learning to belong to healthier systems.

CASE STUDY: SHAMAR

Shamar was in the middle of a job search. He'd recently lost an opportunity with a company he was very excited about because he'd made a major misstep during the interview. He was very embarrassed because he'd done a lot of networking in the process, and had been sharing a lot with colleagues who were closely connected to the company. He felt like his embarrassment and potential incompetence had been made public to everyone he respected. His inclination was to stop reaching out to his network because his ANTs kept telling him, "They're probably sorry they stuck their neck out for me—why would they ever want to vouch for me again?"

But since Shamar is working on his relational resilience, he knows he needs to, one, not hide; two, openly share with those colleagues what happened and what he learned from it; and three, continue building with them. If they have feedback for him, he can practice taking it in and having a growth mindset about it. He can also practice staying nondefensive and being human in his process—both in terms of what he expects from himself and how he expects others to react.

Relational resilience requires several things that are simultaneously helpful to recovering from your impostor syndrome. Relational resilience requires us to address our socially prescribed perfectionism, which allows us to not be perfect in social interactions. When we actively challenge our socially prescribed perfectionism, we recognize that we're allowed to make mistakes in social situations, to not be perfect, to sometimes not even meet others' expectations. And in healthy relationships that will be fine; it won't cause irreparable harm. In addition, it's important for us to learn to talk about our mistakes openly with others—taking appropriate responsibility without obsessing over our error. Last, we must always practice forgiving ourselves, learning, and moving forward when we experience difficult situations

EXERCISE 8.4: PRACTICING RELATIONAL RESILIENCE

The following chart provides some examples of how we can develop relational resilience. Consider which practices might work for you. What are you willing to commit to in order to develop these skills?

SKILL	PRACTICES	YOUR PLAN
Managing strong emotions	Meditation; therapy; processing emotions before reacting to them	
Flexibility	Allowing for a variety of possible outcomes for a situation; pivoting when things don't go as expected	
Communication	Talking about things that are uncomfortable; listening to the full breadth of the conversation—not just the negative parts	
Challenging socially prescribed perfectionism	Allowing for errors in social interactions—for yourself and others	
Trusting and looking for durable, healthy relationships	Believing in the power of relationships—and taking risks to share vulnerabilities; not automatically fearing others' judgment or reaction	
Forgiving yourself	Allowing yourself to have a process around forgiving yourself	

YOUR UNSTOPPABLE GREATNESS

SKILL	PRACTICES	YOUR PLAN
Not dwelling or ruminating about negative situations	Having methods and processes for redirecting your attention to more useful thoughts; understanding that rumination can worsen your perception of the situation	
Mindfulness	Maintaining mindfulness practices aimed at staying present, building resilience, and respecting yourself in your current state	

• • •

Our commitment to practices that will enhance our ability to be present in healthy systems is a reparative process. Understanding that we can learn to discern and decide what systems we want to belong to is powerful. This practice of belonging is critical to helping us avoid the isolation so common to impostor syndrome.

KEY TAKEAWAYS

In closing this chapter, we hope that:

- You've reflected on if and how you tend to remain on the periphery of systems.
- You've learned the components of psychological safety—and how to evaluate the psychological safety of particular systems.
- You've examined how perfectionism may play a role in your ability to fully connect to groups.
- You've become aware of how practicing and being able to be vulnerable can be critical to your work on relationships.
- You've gained knowledge on how to build relational resilience—and how to practice *not* avoiding difficult relational situations.

Chapter 9

CONQUERING LEADERSHIP PITFALLS

We've mentioned how experiencing impostor syndrome can be a double-edged sword in relation to toxic leadership behaviors—both getting triggered by our supervisors and engaging in toxic behaviors when leading others. And so, part of our recovery from impostor syndrome requires that we become conscious of both sides of that sword: the behaviors that reinforce impostor syndrome in ourselves, and also how we reinforce it in others. In this chapter, we'll address the potential leadership pitfalls that are commonly employed by those who struggle with impostor syndrome. We also want to be clear that we use the concept of leadership broadly: we're not (just) referring to if you're someone's manager, supervisor, or boss; we're also referring to any influencing role in which your behavior could impact others, such as mentoring, tutoring, supporting colleagues, even volunteering.

When impostor syndrome has been a part of your life, there are particular pitfalls that you can be vulnerable to when you engage others. As a part of your recovery we want you to be aware of them, to be honest with yourself about when you're using them, and to work on engaging healthier behaviors moving forward. Let's talk through some of the most common of these pitfalls, why they occur, and what we should try to do instead.

MICROMANAGING

Many struggling with impostor syndrome can get preoccupied about both negative evaluation of our own performance and how others' performance may reflect poorly on us. In addition, perfectionism can make us believe the way *we* do things is the "right way"—without realizing that there can be a variety of "best" ways. As a result we can drift into micromanaging, including closely observing and critiquing others' work, being hypercritical and perfectionistic, and being overly involved to the point of intrusion—such as handling work below our position out of requiring the product to look exactly like we'd make it. Micromanaging can be a central culprit in our overworking because our perfectionism can inspire us to do others' jobs as well as our own.

The process of trying to break this habit calls for working on trusting others; providing solid, constructive, and developmental feedback; recognizing that a task can be accomplished well in a multitude of ways, and letting go of tasks that we have mastered but that are actually others' tasks to complete. Micromanaging can be misinterpreted as providing close supervision and supporting others, but it can often feel undermining and distrustful, and leave direct reports and colleagues frustrated, underutilized, and restricted from developing their own process and connection to the work. Moving away from micromanaging behavior requires identifying where it is occurring and considering more adaptive and healthier ways to address the issues. It can be really helpful to ask yourself two questions. One: "Is this really about the task being done well?" If it is, then work on assessing what skills the workers need to develop and how to facilitate that development without intruding or overfunctioning. There's a difference between teaching someone how to fish and repeatedly grabbing the fishing pole. And two, ask: "Is this about me and my insecurities?" If it is, then your task is to discuss with members of your Dream Team the issues related to your discomfort in the role or situation. It might also be the case that you're experiencing a combination of both issues, in which case address them both.

EXERCISE 9.1: REFLECTING ON MICROMANAGING

Take a moment to reflect on your experience. Do you tend to micromanage? If so, do you micromanage everyone? Or do you tend to micromanage particular types of people, such as women, younger employees, or introverted employees? Think about a few specific examples of micromanaging: can you determine what inspires you to micromanage? Are there any specific types of moments that trigger you into micromanaging? Consider what ANTs (automatic negative thoughts) might be at work, such as "They can't handle this, and it will make me look bad." What ANTs come up for you? How might you combat these

ANTs proactively? What commitment can you make to change this behavior? Consider as well what negative impacts your micromanaging might be causing—such as overworking/burnout as well as damaging your relationship with your direct reports.

_____

_____

_____

_____

_____

DELEGATING POORLY

The tendency to micromanage often goes hand in hand with being reluctant to delegate. Impostor syndrome can make it difficult to ascertain what is an appropriate workload and when it's time to allow others to own portions of the work. But it's critical that you learn to delegate, since you likely have responsibilities that only you can complete.

CASE STUDY: ANNA

Anna was a senior manager in a tech company, and she had been assigned a high-profile project. As she reviewed the project she sensed the work was voluminous, but also thought, "My manager wouldn't have assigned it to me if they didn't think I could do it." A few weeks into the project, she was drowning—working late hours and weekends, and yet never feeling she was getting on top of it. She'd also fallen behind on a deadline for more strategic and senior-level work, but had prioritized this project because it was very visible. She was lying low at work because she didn't want anyone asking where the project stood. Her manager eventually checked in with her and asked how the team was doing on the project. Anna was stunned and embarrassed. Not only was she behind on all her responsibilities, she also had to explain why she hadn't engaged the team for the project.

EXERCISE 9.2: ANNA'S DELEGATION SITUATION

Consider the above case study. Why do you imagine Anna didn't engage the team from the beginning? What ANTs might have contributed to her choices? What do you think Anna should tell her manager? What might have she done differently in the beginning?

_____

_____

_____

_____

_____

In our work with employees and leaders who have difficulty with both impostor syndrome and delegation, we've often seen a fear of what will happen if they don't do a project as leanly as possible—with as few resources as possible, so to speak. This applies to projects done either alone or with (very few) others. We know there can be pressure to do this within organizations, but sometimes these ideas come from us as assumptions that we don't think to clarify. It's also true that doing it alone could demonstrate how capable or hardworking we are, so that could be a reason. But we might not realize that choosing not to delegate could send messages we don't intend—such as we're not great at working on or leading a team; we're not clear about our role and responsibilities; we're timid about asking for clarification and guidance; and definitely that we can't manage our workload. This inability to delegate can directly affect how others see us in leadership roles, signaling that we can't manage large teams, scaled projects, or cross-functional work. Of course, those inadvertent messages can greatly impact our chances for additional opportunities and compensation as well as promotion and advancement.

EXERCISE 9.3: REFLECTING ON DELEGATION PRACTICES

Reflect on your own experience with delegation, both when work was delegated to you and when you needed to delegate to others. Here are some questions to consider:

• What are some of the issues that get in the way of your delegation?

• Have you witnessed others engaging in effective delegation?

• Do you struggle with trust?

- Do you have trouble giving feedback that requests a change in behavior?
- Do you jump in too quickly without doing a proper assessment of what resources will be called for?
- Would you prefer to be the sole person acknowledged for achieving a goal?

Is there something else that keeps you from delegating?

_____

_____

_____

_____

_____

_____

Having considered the above, how might you improve your delegation skills? Can you work on practicing trusting others in measured increments? Can you assess what resources you have at your disposal? Can you work on sharing accolades and recognizing others' contributions? Can you work on giving constructive, timely feedback? How might you address sluggish progress? And can you be sure to keep your supervisor apprised along the way?

_____

_____

_____

_____

Changing your experience around delegation can be very difficult. Some struggle with not being familiar with this kind of diluted ownership. But very often the challenge concerns not trusting ourselves as leaders, either because we fear we lack the skills or because we can't imagine others will take us seriously. We can't deny the fact that often what brought about our impostor syndrome was unhealthy leadership—especially our family leadership—and that can often cause us anxiety. If this resonates for you, we want to assure you that your adult professional life is a very different situation from your early home life. Today you're able to take responsibility to make conscious choices about your life and remain aware and accountable. The more consciously you engage in leadership skills, the greater distance you can put between yourself and the unhealthy leadership that you've known.

MODELING OVERWORK

Recovering from and sustaining the gains from conquering impostor syndrome are not overnight experiences. We're trying to break behaviors we've engaged in for almost a lifetime. As a result, some of the behaviors can be so entrenched that we don't even notice them. It can be especially tough to stop overworking because it might seem as though overfunctioning and overproducing has gotten us to where we are today. We might even think, "How do I let go and trust that just working hard will be enough?" As a result, we tend to model overwork—even when we're consciously trying not to. For example, many of our clients and students who are working through their struggles "talk the talk" by advocating work-life balance, self-care, and scheduled time off—but they don't always model those healthier choices. So it's important to recognize that, even if you're making solid recommendations, it's the behaviors you model that have the greatest impact. It's important that the message you send is not: "I value *your* overwork. Look at me—that's how *I* got ahead."

EXERCISE 9.4: AUDITING OVERWORKING BEHAVIOR

Given how deeply entrenched overwork behaviors can be, adjusting them takes time and intentionality. So let's audit how you're currently working. Add checkmarks to the behaviors you engage in, circling specifics as appropriate:

❑ I sometimes/often/always work outside normal business hours on the weekdays.

❑ I sometimes/often/always work on the weekends.

❑ I sometimes/often/always read and send emails and messages outside of business hours.

❑ I sometimes/often/always take on new tasks without first evaluating my workload.

❑ I advertise 24/7 or nearly constant availability.

❑ I sometimes/often/always work during vacation or PTO.

❑ I sometimes/often/always/never take all of my vacation time or PTO.

❑ I sometimes/often/always check work email as my first thing in the morning and my last thing at night.

❑ I sometimes/often/always/never give myself enough time to complete a task.

❑ I sometimes/often/always chime in or get involved in work that's not in my purview.

❑ I _____

What are you learning from doing this audit? What specific behaviors are you open to changing in the near term? For which ones are you going to need more of a long-term plan? What are you actually going to do to change in the short-term? What's your plan for your long-term goals? Who will hold you accountable? How/when will you let them know what you need to support you in this process?

_____

_____

_____

_____

_____

AGONIZING OVER MISTAKES

Making mistakes can be an intense trigger for impostor syndrome, filling us with shame and self-reproach and fear that we've revealed how truly incompetent we are. Unfortunately, many workplace cultures reinforce the penalization of mistake-making. But, even in cultures like these—actually, *especially in cultures like these*—it's critical that you take a different approach. Reorienting ourselves to the meaning of mistake-making is important for our own process as well as for our leadership roles. As we recover, it's essential that our approach to mistakes reflects the fact that mistakes are *human*, inevitable, and ripe for learning. A mistake is a truly potent opportunity: a beautiful moment to teach, to be vulnerable, and to grow—not just for the mistake-maker, but for everyone involved. Everyone should have an opportunity to learn and be given the grace, support, and space to do that learning.

That calls for learning new ways of narrating mistakes and determining what deeper meaning should be applied to us and to others. For example, let's say that when we make a mistake we automatically conclude that we're pathetic and hopeless. The meaning we're attributing to the error is that it just proves we're pathetic and hopeless. Perhaps we think the same of others when they make a mistake. But it's critical that we not approach errors with judgment and assumptions. We must approach mistake-making with openness and curiosity about the process that led to that moment. If we can calmly inquire with the mistake-maker about what happened so as to understand the context of what transpired, we can learn not just how to address that unique situation but also how to broadly apply that learning to other scenarios. In so doing, we can learn as much as we teach in the moment. We can assist the mistake-maker with tools, knowledge, and resources so they can both correct their mistakes and avoid repeating them. It's important to provide feedback along the way, and to offer acknowledgment and rewards as they hit targets in their growth. Being generous in the process of dealing with others' mistakes helps to create a more humane, creative, and community-oriented culture of healthy risk-taking and growth. It also inspires tremendous gratitude and loyalty—all while modeling constructive behavior and actions. That generosity also models to ourselves how to be more self-compassionate, which can encourage us to learn to take more risks.

First, let's identify some of the unproductive, judgmental responses to others' errors that we'd like to remove from our repertoire:

UNCONSTRUCTIVE RESPONSES

- "How could you have done that?"
- "What were you thinking?"
- "What's wrong with you?"
- "Well, that was stupid."
- "Do I have to do everything myself if I want it done right?"
- "You're clearly not ready for the next step."
- "Maybe next time you'll be more thoughtful/work harder/take it more seriously."
- "I can't believe this."

CONSTRUCTIVE RESPONSES

- "Let's start from the beginning. Can you walk me through what led to this point?"

- "Many people struggle with this task. Let's figure out a way to have this work out better next time."
- "Let's focus on our best path forward from here."

CONSTRUCTIVE ACTIONS

- Rather than engaging reactively, give yourself the opportunity to reflect on the mistake, exploring it from a place of curiosity.
- In a considerate, supportive manner, calmly ask the person to relay the details of what happened.
- Offer concrete feedback with examples of how to improve next time.
- For larger situations/projects, break up the goals into reasonable targets so it's clear you're expecting only one step at a time.
- Give them space to correct and follow through on your advice. Don't follow up with them before they've had a reasonable chance to follow through.
- Follow up, offering additional support where needed.
- Provide positive reinforcement for incremental improvement along the way, clearly articulating which behaviors/actions/results you'd like to see more of.
- Consider if you can multiply the benefit by making this a larger teachable moment that others could learn from as well.
- Consider if there are larger issues as to why this mistake happened—and if any training or onboarding changes are called for.

EXERCISE 9.5: TRANSFORMING MISTAKES INTO GROWTH OPPORTUNITIES

Now, think back to a time anyone in your life made a mistake that you had to deal with—one that, upon reflection, you realize you're not completely happy with the way you handled it. Let's consider ways you might have handled it differently.

Describe what happened (the mistake that was made):

_____

_____

_____

Describe your response:

_____

_____

_____

_____

_____

Review the recommendations in the bulleted lists above of possible constructive responses to make. Were this to happen again today, how might you handle this exact scenario so as to maximize a positive outcome?

_____

_____

_____

_____

_____

Consider writing up all the scenarios you can think of that could have been handled better. Thinking about constructive responses now could help you to immediately respond well the next time something happens.

As you work on facilitating a healthier mistake-making process, refer back to the guidelines above so that you can proceed with reflection and intention.

OVERLOOKING CELEBRATORY MOMENTS

The above topic recommends a transparent process that maximizes the potential for not just positive outcomes but also a positive work environment in general. We can keep the positive vibes coming by making the additional effort of sharing with our team moments of acknowledgment, such as an accolade, an award, a promotion, or a change in scope. This applies not just to congratulating the team for their good work but also to sharing the acknowledgment that you personally receive. Oftentimes those who contend with impostor syndrome aren't inclined to toot their own horn, so to speak. In our practice as executive coaches we commonly hear that clients can be reluctant to share celebratory news out of concern for coming off as bragging or being an arrogant narcissist. But as psychologists we also know that those struggling with impostor syndrome are different from those who struggle with narcissism; narcissists are much more likely to believe they're fully deserving of their status and role—not to fear they'll be found out as incapable. Those who contend with impostor syndrome tend to underestimate and underrepresent themselves, which can lead to lost opportunities large and small, of critical moments in your professional life. To follow are some examples of what leveraging a moment might look like—and why we encourage you to do it more often:

Sharing an accolade or special opportunity with others—say, you share with your team that you've won an industry award—presents a different perspective about your skill set and how others value it.

Similarly, sharing news about your hobbies or personal pursuits—like your chorus is giving a concert, or the animal shelter where you volunteer hit an adoption milestone—presents a different perspective about your skill set and interests, which may reveal points of connection.

Shouting out your team or team members—such as when you hit a sales target or team goal and you share it at a town hall—provides them an opportunity to feel proud and get noticed by a broader audience.

Taking the time to spread the good news also models a type of behavior for them which is much more communal and oriented toward a mindset of abundance rather than scarcity. Plus, your sharing a bit of yourself can make others feel closer to you, which can strengthen your relationships.

And when your celebratory news concerns your getting a new job elsewhere, it's important to share it on LinkedIn, since that allows your network and contacts to see your career progression. Putting yourself on others' "radar" makes it more likely they'll think of you when future opportunities present themselves.

EXERCISE 9.6: LEVERAGING MINDSET OPPORTUNITIES

Take some time to consider what moments you could be leveraging better. What are some of your barriers to highlighting these moments? How can you work on lifting those barriers and sharing more with others?

_____

_____

_____

_____

_____

MINIMIZING PERFORMANCE AND CONTRIBUTION

Many who don't leverage important moments also minimize their involvement and value in projects and teams. Though this can come from a place of humility and modesty, it's also connected to one of the hallmarks of impostor syndrome: intellectual inauthenticity. Many don't divulge more of what they know in order to not make others uncomfortable—or because they don't want to reveal their lack of expertise in a subject. You can also engage intellectual inauthenticity when, as a leader, you don't share the accomplishments of team members or their contributions with others for fear of a spotlight being put on them that will reveal their inadequacy or concerns about how others will feel or respond.

It is not a lack of humility to accurately communicate your and your team's contributions. For one thing, it's simply setting the record straight. But it's helping others, especially senior leaders, comprehend where the strengths of the team are, and what kinds of contributions particular people or teams make. It ensures that meaningful contributions receive the proper compensation or accolade they deserve. Not to mention: if you minimize your team's involvement, you may impair their growth and advancement.

EXERCISE 9.7: COMMUNICATING PERFORMANCE AND CONTRIBUTION

Consider in what ways you might be minimizing your or your team's performance or value add. With whom do you need to communicate this value? What are some venues or communities (e.g., with your manager, at a townhall meeting, in online communities) where you could do that? How can you actively change that?

_____

_____

_____

_____

_____

UNDERESTIMATING YOUR VALUE

Periodically we're required to evaluate ourselves in comparison to peers—in more formal situations like performance reviews as well as in informal situations like off-the-cuff conversations with senior leadership. Those of us who struggle with impostor syndrome tend to underestimate ourselves and overestimate others in comparison. As we work on our recovery from impostor syndrome, we'll want to learn how to make more accurate assessments of how our skills, expertise, and competencies rank against others.

Typically, we have no trouble seeing our faults, deficits, and areas in need of improvement. (In fact, research shows that, generally, those with impostor syndrome use negative feedback as an impetus to improve that skill or expertise, often assiduously.[45]) We do have trouble identifying our strengths and areas of expertise, especially when comparing our efforts against those of our peers or laterals (those on the same level). So it can help to initially lean on people we trust to be honest (but also positive) evaluators of the realm of expertise in question. This is where healthy mentors and senior colleagues can be very helpful. We just want to make sure they can talk about your strengths in concrete terms speaking to your distinct behaviors and actions so that it's clear what you're actually good at, and that they'll readily give honestly earned positive feedback—and aren't pessimistic perfectionists themselves. This entire process can be difficult for us because many of us are uncomfortable with positive feedback. In fact, this is a time when the "Discounting Positives" ANT can kick in, so pay particular attention to defeating this ANT.

Be sure to ask your mentors and knowledgeable "cheerleaders" to help you *articulate* your strengths. This is especially important in relation to your leadership of a team. If you underestimate yourself as a leader and/or downplay your success as a team, you might accidentally imply that your team is underperforming, which of course would affect their prospects as well as yours. One last item: be sure to ask your mentors and cheerleaders how you can maximize and leverage your strengths.

EXERCISE 9.8: ACCURATELY ASSESSING YOUR STRENGTHS

Part 1: Identify three people who qualify as a healthy mentor or "cheerleader" in your field.

1. _____

2. _____

3. _____

Part 2: Ask them to discuss with you three of your strengths, including how you compare against your peers—with behavioral examples if possible.

Ask them to help you articulate those strengths.

Ask them to help you maximize and leverage those strengths.

Document all that you discuss.

Part 3: Practice how you will articulate your strengths to others.

_____

_____

_____

_____

_____

Part 4: Revisit the assessments your mentors provided. How do both versions compare—are you still downplaying your strengths? If so, why? How can you work to appreciate and think of yourself more favorably and accurately? What is the difference between how you evaluate yourself and how your mentors viewed you? Can you adapt your assessment by adopting some of their appraisal?

_____

_____

_____

DEALING WITH NEGATIVE STEREOTYPES

Stereotypes about identity groups (e.g., race, gender, ability) that you belong to can significantly and unfairly affect your influence and leadership. Add to which, discriminatory treatment can trigger impostor syndrome, cueing the standard worries and fears. Indeed, research has shown that individuals with impostor syndrome can be more aware of and influenced by the stereotypes of their groups.[46] If you experience this, it's important to note the concept of stereotype threat that we discussed in *Own Your Greatness*. Some groups are often stereotyped, such as being "not expressive enough" or "quick to anger." It's all too easy to either slip into those stereotypical behaviors or to overcompensate by engaging in the opposite behavior. As painful as that experience is, try to remember that you don't need to prove yourself—you just need to be your authentic self.

CASE STUDY: LISA (continued from page 130)

Lisa had a manager who'd started her career in the seventies and eighties. This manager faced a significant amount of prejudice against her as a woman and had some public conflicts competing with men for leadership positions—and losing. She wasn't able to properly process these painful struggles. As a result, she had internalized a lot of the toxicity she'd experienced, and it showed up in her leadership. She was very difficult with pregnant women in particular; she often cut them off from key projects because she knew "they would be gone soon." She also cut them off emotionally, progressively distancing herself from them. She had a great deal of difficulty handling conflict among women;

she blamed them for their behavior and marginalized them further. However, she offered significantly more latitude to men who were problematic; they did whatever they liked.

If you experience prejudicial behavior toward you and your leadership, it's very important that you develop deep community in your identity groups in your profession. It's also important to watch for when you're triggered, and to be sure to respond consciously, not automatically. In addition, we recommend you actively process the microaggressions you regularly experience so you don't internalize them or endure them alone. A therapist or coach can be essential in helping you manage the effects of microaggressions, prejudice, and discrimination and guiding you in considering how to strategically address these forms of oppression.

EXERCISE 9.9: REFLECTING ON STEREOTYPE TRAPS

Take a moment to reflect on the ways that stereotypes about your identities (e.g., gender, race, sexual orientation, and so on) have affected the ways that you show up at work. For example, if you worked in a male-dominated profession that had stereotypes about women being less effective due to their gender, you may have felt that you couldn't be your authentic self for fear that you would be viewed negatively.

_____

_____

_____

_____

_____

_____

_____

PERPETUATING THE MYTH OF EXECUTIVE PRESENCE

An unfortunate reality that we've often seen obstructing the expansion of diversity in leadership is the idea of "executive presence"—wherein the candidates hired for executive positions are those who visually match those already in such positions: namely, White men. This can be especially problematic when those making hiring decisions can't articulate precisely what they're looking for. As you become a healthy leader, make sure that you don't engage in these kinds of offensive and discriminatory notions that serve as "gatekeeping" to those who can't access leadership. Once we're in the position of hiring leadership, it's essential that we clearly articulate all the specific behaviors and skills needed for the position (e.g., business development, public speaking, management of large groups, strategy) in the job description. We cannot assume that certain attributes are innately possessed by a certain type of person; everything in a posted job description can be learned and developed.

And as for hiring from within, an organization should provide opportunities to established employees to develop the skills needed for the more senior-level positions. So, as you develop in your leadership and have increasing organizational influence, make sure that you're doing just that: clarify what skills are needed at higher levels, and give those junior to you the opportunity to develop and practice those skills, perhaps in a "scaffolding" manner—with skilled supervision guiding the learning in house. Too often it is assumed that leadership skills are either innate or almost atmospherically learned along the way, but neither is true. Sadly, this mindset can lead to internal promotions and hiring decisions allowing candidates to "try out" leadership without proper training, supervision, and guidance, which can result in their struggle to maintain those positions. This experimentation without support can be ineffective. It is critical that we develop leadership properly and thoughtfully.

EXERCISE 9.10: REFLECTING ON GATEKEEPING

Be honest with yourself in this exercise and examine what you expect in a leader (e.g., What does a leader look like? What are their qualities and credentials? How do they present themselves?) You can do this also by reflecting on some of your favorite leaders so it's less abstract. How can you challenge any of the notions that may be biased or limit who may be considered a leader?

LEADERSHIP PREFERENCES	AREAS FOR CHALLENGE

KEY TAKEAWAYS

In closing this chapter, we hope that:

- You have a strong understanding of the possible leadership pitfalls that may affect you.
- You've examined how you might be engaging in each of the potential pitfalls, and now know how to create healthier outcomes.
- You've reflected on the ways your impostor syndrome can negatively impact others, and now know how you can work to eliminate those behaviors.
- You understand how the stereotypes related to your identity impact your experience of leadership.

Chapter 10

DEVELOPING HEALTHY LEADERSHIP

Now that we've examined the leadership pitfalls driven by impostor syndrome, let's look at how we can orient ourselves as healthy leaders in an organization. (Note that by "leaders" we mean anyone who contributes to the dynamics of an organization.) We'll want to work proactively to lead and model leadership in ways that help others to own their greatness and feel freedom in their success.

CREATING PSYCHOLOGICAL SAFETY

We discussed psychological safety earlier in the book; now we're going to apply it directly to how you engage and lead at work. Feeling that you have psychological safety means you feel able to share yourself without experiencing negative consequences. Creating a psychologically safe environment in turn requires leadership that allows others to feel free to be *themselves*. So we want to identify the ways impostor syndrome can threaten that safety in order to ensure that we neither become a toxic boss or produce toxic bosses.

CONSISTENTLY OFFER PRAISE AND FEEDBACK

You're no doubt familiar with how those with impostor syndrome can regularly withhold positive feedback and then only offer praise for stellar work. We'll want to move away from this mindset, since employees left guessing how their performance is being judged creates an unhealthy atmosphere. Humans are wired to respond positively to positive feedback—especially for being seen and being validated for what they are doing well. And so creating psychological safety for your team calls for clarifying precisely what is expected of them, and consistently sharing feedback—especially praise and reward. Consistent feedback means we don't just praise the successful conclusion of a large project. This calls for commenting on small, incremental efforts; we need to learn how to notice and praise all the micro accomplishments made along the way. In other words, we need to appreciate the process, not just the outcome. The process is as important as the outcome. The process is where the teaching and learning can happen, and it deserves respect.

LEAD FROM A PLACE OF TRUSTING YOUR TEAM

Another angle of this concerns moving away from the "prove it to me" stance—where employees feel pressured to demonstrate excellence in order to be seen at all. This viewpoint of course can trigger insecurity in team members and inspire overworking—especially in marginalized groups, who can feel they need to prove even more than the others do. We'll want to work with the assumption that those who have been hired into our institution have clearly demonstrated that they're competent and so are deserving of that respect. This isn't to say keep quiet and trust (and hope); since it's important to provide regular feedback, we're already in a position to address issues when they arise. This is to say trust in others from the foundational belief that they are competent and will come through. An additional benefit is that this approach also supports diversity, equity, and inclusion practices.

PROMOTE EXCELLENCE-IN-PROGRESS, NOT PERFECTIONISM

As we proactively work on our recovery, we want to move away from the notion that perfectionism is the path to success, since we know that perfectionism contracts people, making them fearful, anxious, and prone to burnout. We want to instead focus on creativity, growth, taking risks in safe spaces, learning from mistakes, and progress. These efforts apply to both you individually and to what you promote for those working with you.

That said, we want to make a note about the perfectionistic nature of professions like engineering, architecture, mathematics, accounting, finance, dance, medicine, law, and so many others. Yes, it's true that a building built from a flawed design could collapse, but we're not advocating sloppy, incomplete work. It's possible for the expectations around tasks to be *exacting* without including the harmful elements of perfectionistic culture, such as punishing errors and vilifying those who aren't perfect—especially since none of us is perfect. We recommend promoting excellent work from within an environment that nurtures open, curious, and supportive learning and development.

CHAMPION INCLUSIVE, SAFE ENVIRONMENTS—NO BULLIES ALLOWED

Healthy leadership calls for championing inclusive environments where everyone is welcome—and where there is zero tolerance for behaviors that are in any way unsupportive, bullying, aggressive, or toxic, including hazing and gatekeeping. Should you encounter this behavior with direct reports, peers, or even senior leaders, you'll first want to make it clear that it is absolutely unacceptable. Second, it's important to investigate it further so you can identify the full extent of it, provide support to those who were victim to it, and implement a remediation plan for the aggressor(s), including clear targets and goals and an evaluation of their progress. Also be sure not to ever make excuses for harmful behavior, such as saying the provoking party is stressed, or because they're otherwise "a good person." There is never an excuse for abusive behavior—and the best way to advertise that is to never support it in any way, whether actively and explicitly or passively and implicitly.

FOCUS ON DEVELOPING ALL EMPLOYEES

A healthy leader focuses on growing and developing all employees, especially the ones who are struggling. It's very common to focus on only the high performers—and to write off the poor performers, perhaps deeming their "issues" to be inherent and unfixable. This is especially important since modeling writing people off sends the message to everyone: "You screw up and you're done—this could be you." Your job as a leader is to do whatever you can to support those who work for you so they can contribute to the organization's success.

As an aside, be aware of signs that you're engaging in affinity bias, which is offering preferential treatment for people who are similar to you. Again, the point is to develop *all* employees.

PREVENT ORGANIZATION-DRIVEN BURNOUT

As we discussed, reducing and preventing burnout takes both individual and organizational efforts. However, organizations and leaders are the key drivers in terms of creating a genuinely burnout-free work culture. In order for burnout to truly be dramatically reduced, organizations and their managers need to do a much better job of creating work environments that do the following to prevent higher incidence of burnout:

Respect employees' time and energy: Frequent interruptions and unnecessary meetings can definitely drain one's energy. Further, the risk of burnout tends to increase when employees work over 50 hours. Therefore, managers should be mindful of the time pressures they are exerting on employees for specific deadlines, as well as be mindful about how many hours their employees are actually working.

Clearly identify work responsibilities and priorities: Most employees want clear instructions about their work duties and priorities, in order to focus their efforts and plan their work days. By being vague about what an employee's work responsibilities and high-level priorities are, managers can cause undue stress, confusion, and overwork, which lead to higher levels of burnout.

Right size positions: Make sure that positions are appropriately scoped for the designated amount of time that the employee is working and not more than that. When you consistently add responsibilities to an employee's job description, without eliminating any duties, the job will become outsized and lead to employee burnout.

Support self-care: Model and support employees taking their PTO and vacation time as well as their sick leave when they need it. Wellness benefits (e.g., gym membership, massages, therapy) should be part of their benefits package, and if they are, you should encourage your employees to use them. You should also support employees to have full lives outside of work.

Provide employees with a greater sense of autonomy: The more employees feel that they have control over their work duties, the more engaged and less prone to burnout they will be, even if they are working more hours. Managers should avoid micromanaging and allow their employees to clearly set their plans for completing projects and assignments, with consistent communication among all parties involved.

Listen to work-related problems: A 2019 Gallup study found that employees who said that their managers listen to their work-related problems were 62 percent less likely to experience burnout.[47] So make sure to schedule regular check-in time with your direct reports to explore their challenges.

Attend to any gaps in employee burnout: Different groups of employees (e.g., manager, front-line staff, direct service employees) may experience burnout at higher levels. For instance, prior to the pandemic, in 2019, 30 percent of women and 27 percent of men said that they experienced burnout "Always" or "Very Often." In 2021, the gender gap increased to 8 percent, with 34 percent of women reporting those levels of burnout versus 26 percent of men.[48] By recognizing trends in employee burnout and possible gaps, companies can evaluate the reasons for these gaps and concentrate their resources on particular groups or interventions to eliminate them.

Be aware of how work subject matter affects employees: It's important to remember that if you are working with or for certain populations such as those with decreased resources, increased trauma, and urgent or emergency situations, your employees may be more susceptible to burnout or vicarious trauma (e.g., being traumatized by exposure to the content), which can lead to burnout. Therefore, provide resources and spaces for employees to process some of the challenges of their roles to help them reduce the possibility of burnout.

EXERCISE 10.1: DEVELOPING PSYCHOLOGICALLY SAFE LEADERSHIP

Take a moment to reflect on the different components of psychological safety in the workplace. For each component, consider at least one behavior you can begin to engage in.

PSYCHOLOGICAL SAFETY COMPONENT	ACTION YOU WILL TAKE
Consistently offer praise and feedback.	
Lead from a place of trusting your team.	
Promote excellence-in-progress, not perfectionism.	
Champion inclusive, safe environments.	
Focus on developing all employees	
Prevent organizational burnout	

• • •

BUILDING YOUR TEAM

As you grow in your career, building a team will be a part of your everyday leadership activities. Doing so with intention and clear purpose will help to institute team-development practices that foster a healthy work environment—not one that triggers impostor syndrome behaviors. To follow are guidelines for building a strong team.

INSIST ON DIVERSE HIRING POOLS

We've discussed in earlier chapters that a commitment to DEI is central to creating healthy work environments. When we focus on developing workforces where everyone is welcomed and supported, and where unique strengths and styles are valued, we have the opportunity to benefit from divergent viewpoints, experiences, and orientations—which fosters moving away from the conformity of groupthink in favor of facilitating the generation of unique, viable solutions to problems.

DEI best practices begin with fair and unbiased processes aimed at rooting out any cultural behaviors that lean toward similarity and rigidity. To this end, we want to reduce the impact of both conscious and unconscious (implicit) bias. Studies have shown that even the most enlightened and intentional among us are influenced by implicit bias; its effect cannot be underestimated. (For more, please visit the Project Implicit website.)[49]

For example:

Review résumés blind. Remove names and identifying information from résumés so reviewers can't apply any conscious or unconscious bias.

Reduce bias in interviews. Interviews can be rife for bias since interviewers can ask whatever they want and evaluate the responses however they like. So make sure that the open positions' job descriptions advertise the required set of qualifications and competencies—and that the interview questions are aimed at assessing them. Interview rubrics can provide guidelines for both the phrasing of interview questions and the answers to look for, plus how to score the responses. (See also the "Culture Fit" topic lower down.)

Address bias issues when they occur. Watch for behaviors like "mansplaining," when the comments made by a woman need to be reiterated by a man in order to be considered, and "whitesplaining," when the comments made by a person of color need to be reiterated by a White person in order to be considered. Similarly, be on the lookout for individuals from privileged groups getting the credit for work or ideas contributed—sometimes from the background—by those from historically marginalized groups.

Support diverse representation on your teams. This is especially important in relation to visibility and leadership.

Watch out for double standards. Call it out when people from different groups are treated differently—especially in relation to privilege.

DIVERSIFY THE "CULTURE FIT" CONCEPT

"Culture fit" can be code for tolerating bias against difference in the name of everyone working together well. You'll want to move away from subjective notions concerning who is qualified to be hired or participate on a team. If you're looking for specific relational or interpersonal skills, then explicitly state that you seek openness and productive collaboration, communication, and listening skills. Also, broadcast this policy to your entire organization. If people on your team use the term "culture fit" to exclude or even include people, start by telling them that this global term isn't appropriate. Then, after hearing what skills and competencies they're referring to—and after ensuring you approve of specifying those qualities—remind them of the inclusivity approach specified in your policy.

ASSESS HOW PROJECTS ARE ASSIGNED

It's important to be very intentional about how projects are assigned and how teams are created. This is in part to continue the policies of inclusivity and diversity—especially for visible projects. But it's also to ensure that developmental opportunities are available to all employees, as noted in the Focus on Developing All Employees topic above. Reflect on anyone who may be hiding from or ignoring visibility and ensure their growth with appropriate supervision and support.

ENSURE EQUITABLE ACCESS TO YOU AND SENIOR LEADERSHIP

As you develop your team, it's important to support different styles of engaging leadership. Some people are very comfortable accessing leadership and readily reach out for informal conversations that can lead to more meaningful relationships, premium assignments, and hidden opportunities. And then there are those steeped in impostor syndrome who are reluctant to engage, perhaps with the hope that they'll be noticed, acknowledged, and rewarded solely from their hard work and achievement. But we know all too well it doesn't always work this way. So it's essential to ensure that all employees, especially those not practiced in strategic interpersonal skills, get equal access to opportunities for growth. Check in on a regular basis with all those who avoid the limelight. Teach them how to build relationships with "skip levels"—meaning, the leader above you = your boss. (For that, see Teaching Direct Reports How to Engage Skip Levels below.)

TEACHING DIRECT REPORTS HOW TO ENGAGE SKIP LEVELS

- Communicate the value of the skip-level relationship.
- Share how your manager likes to engage, especially during skip-level meetings.
- Prep them for skip-level meetings, especially the first one, including the intended goal of the meeting and how long it will likely be.
- Support them in processing and developing solutions to any issues that may arise.

WATCH FOR CLIQUES AND UNSUPPORTIVE TEAM BEHAVIOR

This is the mild variation of the bullying behaviors discussed earlier. Of course, team members will develop friendships with some but not others. However, it is problematic when friend groups develop into cliques that then can become a power bloc—a group of people who can assert their will due to having several people automatically on their side, such as in a team vote on an important decision that affects everyone. As a leader it can be hard to see where this is occurring, especially if it happens outside of work. But you can watch group dynamics in meetings, and make note of whose ideas come to the surface and get supported—versus whose ideas do not. For guidance on how best to break up alliances meant to ostracize and deauthorize other team members, consider mixing up who is working on projects together so people can obtain greater exposure to new or other people; directly address any toxic behavior; listen to all voices; and model, teach, and reinforce inclusive behavior.

CHANNEL DISAGREEMENT AND CONFLICT INTO PRODUCTIVE DISCUSSION

Naturally, you'll want to support healthy group dynamics whenever possible. And while conflict and disagreement are a normal part of the development of any team, they can become opportunities for growth and even team strengthening if they're handled thoughtfully, respectfully, and productively. Working through dissent and disagreement can advance a team to far beyond what either side brought to the table. This calls for finding ways of mediating issues that, one, teach your employees how to see such situations in a more positive, productive light; and, two, broaden your employees' methods of handling them. The goal is to process disagreement such that it brings about the change that's being called for. Facilitating healthy conflict calls for the following:

- Choosing a space that is conducive to productive conversation.
- Establishing boundaries up front: setting a time limit, as appropriate; and agreeing to rules of engagement, such as not permitting disrespect, especially name-calling.
- Committing to speaking in a calm, grounded conversational style.
- Being willing to actively listen—using paraphrasing, reflecting, and summarization skills; an openness to understanding someone else's point. (For more, see the Active Listening Techniques sidebar.)
- Committing to neither taking "things" personally nor reacting defensively.
- Being willing to take responsibility and accountability, as appropriate.
- Ensuring that, when the conversation ends, everyone is on the same page regarding the problem, possible solutions, and next steps.

ACTIVE LISTENING TECHNIQUES

Attending behavior: Demonstrate your receptivity with attentive body language like making eye contact and leaning forward; make sure your arms are at your sides, not crossed over your chest.

Open-ended questions: Ask questions that illicit more than a "yes" or "no" response. Allow the person to elaborate; ask exploratory questions that are not accusatory but rather curious and inquisitive.

Paraphrasing: Empathetically respond to the person: repeat what you heard, focusing on feelings and what's important to them. If you're in doubt, don't assume—just ask if you heard them correctly.

Clarifying: Request clarification on any points you don't quite understand.

Summarizing: As the conversation is winding down, sum it up—specifying any follow-up or action items.

EXERCISE 10.2: **BUILDING YOUR TEAM**

Take a moment to reflect on each component discussed in this section. For each component, consider at least one behavior you can begin to engage in.

TEAM-BUILDING COMPONENT	ACTION YOU WILL TAKE
Insist on diverse hiring pools.	
Diversify the "culture fit" concept.	
Assess how projects are assigned.	
Ensure equitable access to you and senior leadership.	
Watch for cliques and unsupportive team behavior.	
Channel disagreement and conflict into productive discussion.	

• • •

In closing this chapter, we hope that:

- You've begun to reflect on the various aspects of leadership you want to embody.
- You've contemplated and mapped (or begun mapping) how you will create psychological safety in your organization—including how to prevent or break up toxicity on your teams.
- You've contemplated and mapped (or begun mapping) how you want to consciously build your team.
- You'll remember to revisit this chapter when you feel disconnected from your leadership or feel you need to rethink how things are functioning.

CONCLUSION: YOUR UNSTOPPABLE GREATNESS

Our first book, *Own Your Greatness*, provided the key components to defeating impostor syndrome. In this book, *Your Unstoppable Greatness*, we presented the 3 A's model of Agency, Assessment, and Actualization, which will enable you to break from impostor syndrome, counter it should it reemerge, and actively respond to the toxic work cultures that sustain it. Insight on how to reduce impostor syndrome within organizations enables you to take direct action to protect yourself *and* change the system. We encourage you to practice and grow so that you can apply all you've learned to changing any toxic systems you encounter. All of us need healthy workplaces where we can express and develop our talents and share our expertise. We also need systems that not only *don't* perpetuate impostor syndrome but that also work to eradicate it—so that employees can feel safe to both fully actualize professionally and own their unstoppable greatness.

As we conclude, it's important to revisit the process of cultivating your agency, assessing your reality, and actualizing your break from impostor syndrome—all so that you can take ownership of your unstoppable greatness and achieve your ultimate career goals.

Agency is about connecting or reconnecting to your dreams, envisioning them, and protecting them. By managing and preventing burnout and working on your perfectionism, you're well on the road to achieving your dreams.

Assessment is about examining how your early childhood and familial relationships may have set unhealthy, familiar patterns that established a vulnerability to these types of relationships and cultures in your work life. By considering ways to break from these patterns, you give yourself the opportunity to choose better leaders and healthier environments.

Actualization is about putting into action what you've learned so that you can be a healthier leader and can push for workplace dynamics that enable everyone to be their authentic and best selves.

We are so proud of you for reaching this point in your journey to break free of impostor syndrome. We have been honored to take this journey with you and know that you are ready to step into your unstoppable greatness now and for years to come.

NOTES

1 Lisa Orbé-Austin and Richard Orbé-Austin, "The Impostor Syndrome Paradox: Unleashing the Power of You," TEDxDeerPark, March 23, 2000, 12:13, https://www.youtube.com/watch?v=u2zbcZBI0Do.

2 Bureau of Labor Statistics, US Department of Labor, The Economics Daily, "Median Tenure with Current Employer Was 4.1 Years in January 2020," September 29, 2020, https://www.bls.gov/opub/ted/2020/median-tenure-with-current-employer-was-4-point-1-years-in-january-2020.htm.

3 Cameron Keng, "Employees Who Stay in Companies Longer Than Two Years Get Paid 50% Less," *Forbes*, June 22, 2014, https://www.forbes.com/sites/cameronkeng/2014/06/22/employees-that-stay-in-companies-longer-than-2-years-get-paid-50-less/?sh=2a94063ee07f.

4 Ben Wigert, "How to Eliminate Burnout and Retain Top Talent," Gallup, August 25, 2021, https://www.gallup.com/workplace/353831/eliminate-burnout-retain-top-talent.aspx; Ben Wigert and Sangeeta Agrawal, "Employee Burnout, Part 1: The 5 Main Causes," Gallup, July 12, 2018, https://www.gallup.com/workplace/237059/employee-burnout-part-main-causes.aspx.

5 Lydia Saad, Sangeeta Agrawal, and Ben Wigert, "Gender Gap in Worker Burnout Widened During the Pandemic," Gallup, December 27, 2021, https://www.gallup.com/workplace/358349/gender-gap-worker-burnout-widened-amid-pandemic.aspx.

6 World Health Organization, "Burn-Out an 'Occupational Phenomenon': International Classification of Diseases," May 28, 2019, https://www.who.int/news/item/28-05-2019-burn-out-an-occupational-phenomenon-international-classification-of-diseases.

7 World Health Organization, 2019 (see note 6).

8 Wigert, "How to Eliminate Burnout" (see note 4).

9 Eric Garton, "Employee Burnout Is a Problem with the Company, Not the Person," *Harvard Business Review*, April 06, 2017, https://hbr.org/2017/04/employee-burnout-is-a-problem-with-the-company-not-the-person. See also Michael C. Mankins and Eric Garton, *Time, Talent, Energy: Overcome Organizational Drag and Unleash Your Team's Productive Power* (Boston: Harvard Business Review Press, 2017).

10 P. Hewitt and G. Flett, "Perfectionism in the Self and Social Contexts: Conceptualization, Assessment, and Association with Psychopathology," *Journal of Personality and Social Psychology* 60, no. 3 (March 1991): 456–70, https://doi.org/10.1037//0022-3514.60.3.456.

11 T. Curran and A. Hill, "Perfectionism Is Increasing Over Time: A Meta-Analysis of Birth Cohort Differences from 1989 to 2016," *Psychological Bulletin* 145, no. 4 (2019): 410–29, https://doi.org/10.1037/bul0000138.

12 Brian Swider, Dana Harari, Amy P. Breidenthal, and Laurens Bujold Steed, "The Pros and Cons of Perfectionism, According to Research," *Harvard Business Review*, December 27, 2018, https://hbr.org/2018/12/the-pros-and-cons-of-perfectionism-according-to-research.

13 Carol S. Dweck, *Mindset: The New Psychology of Success* (New York: Random House, 2006).

14 Merriam-Webster.com Dictionary, s.v. "system," accessed May 5, 2022, https://www.merriam-webster.com/dictionary/system.

15 Michael E. Kerr and Murray Bowen, *Family Evaluation* (New York and London: W. W. Norton, 1988), 9–11.

16 S. Tripathi and P. Jadon, "Effect of Authoritarian Parenting Style on Self-Esteem of the Child: A Systematic Review," *International Journal of Advanced Research and Innovative Ideas* 3 (2017): 909–13.

17 "Narcissus," *Encyclopedia Britannica*, https://www.britannica.com/topic/Narcissus-Greek-mythology.

18 Donald Sull, Charles Sull, and Ben Zweig, "Toxic Culture Is Driving the Great Resignation," *MIT Sloan Management Review*, January 11, 2022, https://sloanreview.mit.edu/article/toxic-culture-is-driving-the-great-resignation. In the same journal see also Donald Sull, Charles Sull, William Cipolli, and Caio Brighenti, "Why Every Leader Needs to Worry About Toxic Culture," https://sloanreview.mit.edu/article/why-every-leader-needs-to-worry-about-toxic-culture.

19 Ruth Namie and Gary Namie, 2021 WBI Workplace Bullying Survey, "2. The Affected U.S. Workforce" (https://workplacebullying.org/wp-content/uploads/2021/03/2.-Affected.pdf) and "6. Rank of Perpetrators" (https://workplacebullying.org/wp-content/uploads/2021/03/6.-Rank-Perp.pdf), Workplace Bullying Institute, n.d., accessed June 3, 2022.

20 Steve Bates, "Forced Ranking," *HR Magazine*, June 1, 2003, https://www.shrm.org/hr-today/news/hr-magazine/pages/0603bates.aspx.

21 Tripathi and Jadon, "Effect of Authoritarian Parenting Style" (see note 16).

22 T. C. Rothrauff et al., "Remembered Parenting Styles and Adjustment in Middle and Late Adulthood," *Journals of Gerontology Series B* 64B, no. 1 (2009): 137–46, https://doi.org/10.1093/geronb/gbn008.

23 Leading Effectively Staff, "Master the 3 Ways to Influence People," Center for Creative Leadership, November 24, 2020, https://www.ccl.org/articles/leading-effectively-articles/three-ways-to-influence-people.

24 W. Kahn and K. Kram, "Authority at Work: Internal Models and Their Organizational Consequences," *Academy of Management Review* 19, no. 1 (1994): 17–50, https://doi.org/10.2307/258834.

25 L. McGregor et al., "I Feel Like a Fraud and It Depresses Me: The Relation between the Imposter Phenomenon and Depression," *Social Behavior and Personality* 36, no. 1 (2008): 43–48, https://doi.org/10.2224/sbp.2008.36.1.43.

26 D. M. Szymanski and M. R. Sung, "Minority Stress and Psychological Distress among Asian American Sexual Minority Persons," *Counseling Psychologist* 38, no. 6 (2010): 848–72, https://doi .org/10.1177/0011000010366167.

27 K. Cokley et al., "An Examination of the Impact of Minority Status Stress and Impostor Feelings on the Mental Health of Diverse Ethnic Minority College Students," *Journal of Multicultural Counseling and Development* 41, no. 2 (2013): 82–95, https://doi.org/10.1002/j.2161-1912.2013.00029.x.

28 C. Austin et al., "Impostorism as a Mediator between Survivor Guilt and Depression in a Sample of African American College Students," *College Student Journal* 43 (2009): 1094–1109; D. L. Bernard et al., "Racial Discrimination, Racial Identity, and Impostor Phenomenon: A Profile Approach," *Cultural Diversity and Ethnic Minority Psychology* 24, no. 1 (2018): 51, https://doi.org/10.1037 /cdp0000161.

29 K. Cokley et al., "Impostor Feelings as a Moderator and Mediator of the Relationship between Perceived Discrimination and Mental Health among Racial/Ethnic Minority College Students," *Journal of Counseling Psychology* 64, no. 2 (2017): 141, https://doi.org/10.1037/cou0000198.

30 Cokley et al., "Examination of the Impact," 2013 (see note 33); Cokley et al., "Impostor Feelings," 2017 (see note 35).

31 A. Atkin et al., "Internalization of the Model Minority Myth, School Racial Composition, and Psychological Distress among Asian American Adolescents," *Asian American Journal of Psychology* 9, no. 2 (2018): 108, https://doi.org/10.1037/aap0000096.

32 M. Wei et al., "Impostor Feelings and Psychological Distress among Asian Americans: Interpersonal Shame and Self-Compassion," *Counseling Psychologist* 48, no. 3 (2020): 432–58, https://doi.org/10.1177/0011000019891992.

33 C. Holden et al., "Imposter Syndrome among First- and Continuing-Generation College Students: The Roles of Perfectionism and Stress," *Journal of College Student Retention* (2021): https://doi .org/10.1177/15210251211019379.

34 E. Canning et al., "Feeling Like an Imposter: The Effect of Perceived Classroom Competition on the Daily Psychological Experiences of First-Generation College Students," *Social Psychological and Personality Science* 11, no. 5 (2020): 647–57, https://doi.org/10.1177/1948550619882032.

35 Pauline Rose Clance, quoted in L.V. Anderson, "Feeling Like an Impostor Is Not a Syndrome," *Slate*, April 12, 2016, https://slate.com/business/2016/04/is-impostor-syndrome-real-and-does-it -affect-women-more-than-men.html. Note that Clance and Imes are considered the cofounders of the impostor "phenomenon."

36 C. Cusack et al., "Connecting Gender and Mental Health to Imposter Phenomenon Feelings," *Psi Chi* 18, no. 2 (2013): 74–81, https://doi.org/10.24839/2164-8204.JN18.2.74; G. Jöstl et al., "When Will They Blow My Cover? The Impostor Phenomenon among Austrian Doctoral Students," *Zeitschrift für Psychologie* 220, no. 2 (2012): 109–20, https://doi.org/10.1027/2151-2604/a000102.

37 L. Blondeau and G. Awad, "The Relation of the Impostor Phenomenon to Future Intentions of Mathematics-Related School and Work," *Journal of Career Development* 45, no. 3 (2018): 253–67, https://doi.org/10.1177/0894845316680769.

38 A. Patzak et al., "Buffering Impostor Feelings with Kindness: The Mediating Role of Self-Compassion between Gender-Role Orientation and the Impostor Phenomenon," *Frontiers in Psychology* 8 (2017): 1289, https://doi.org/10.3389/fpsyg.2017.01289.

39 K. Cokley et al., "The Roles of Gender Stigma Consciousness, Impostor Phenomenon and Academic Self-Concept in the Academic Outcomes of Women and Men," *Sex Roles: A Journal of Research* 73, nos. 9–10 (2015): 414–26, https://doi.org/10.1007/s11199-015-0516-7.

40 S. Kumar and C. Jagacinski, "Imposters Have Goals Too: The Imposter Phenomenon and Its Relationship to Achievement Goal Theory," *Personality and Individual Differences* 40, no. 1 (2006): 147–57, https://doi.org/10.1016/j.paid.2005.05.014; M. Neureiter and E. Traut-Mattausch, "An Inner Barrier to Career Development: Preconditions of the Impostor Phenomenon and Consequences for Career Development," *Frontiers in Psychology* 7 (2016): 48, https://doi.org/10.3389/fpsyg.2016.00048.

41 A. Edmondson, "Psychological Safety and Learning Behavior in Work Teams," *Administrative Science Quarterly* 44, no. 2 (1999): 350–83, https://doi.org/10.2307/2666999.

42 Markus Baer and Michael Frese, "Innovation Is Not Enough: Climates for Initiative and Psychological Safety, Process Innovations, and Firm Performance," *Journal of Organizational Behavior* 24, no. 1 (2003): 45–68, https://doi.org/10.1002/job.179; Amy Edmondson and Bertrand Moingeon, "Learning, Trust and Organizational Change: Contrasting Models of Intervention Research in Organizational Behavior," in *Organizational Learning and the Learning Organization: Developments in Theory and Practice*, ed. Mark Easterby-Smith, Luis Araujo, and John G. Burgoyne (London: Sage Publications, 1999), 157–75; R. Kark and A. Carmeli, "Alive and Creating: The Mediating Role of Vitality and Aliveness in the Relationship between Psychological Safety and Creative Work Involvement," *Journal of Organizational Behavior* 30, no. 6 (2009): 785–804, https://doi.org/10.1002/job.571.

43 Aaron De Smet, Kim Rubenstein, Gunnar Schrah, Mike Vierow, and Amy Edmondson, "Psychological Safety and the Critical Role of Leadership Development," McKinsey & Company, February 11, 2021, https://www.mckinsey.com/business-functions/people-and-organizational-performance/our-insights/psychological-safety-and-the-critical-role-of-leadership-development.

44 MasterClass staff, "Positive Conflict: 4 Benefits of Positive Conflict in the Workplace," last updated April 13, 2022, https://www.masterclass.com/articles/positive-conflict#what-is-positive-conflict.

45 R. Badawy et al., "Are All Impostors Created Equal? Exploring Gender Differences in the Impostor Phenomenon-Performance Link," *Personality and Individual Differences* 131 (2018): 156–63, https://doi.org/10.1016/j.paid.2018.04.044.

46 Cokley et al., "Roles of Gender Stigma Consciousness" (see note 45).

47 Saad, Lydia, Sangeeta Agrawal, and Ben Wigert. "Gender Gap in Worker Burnout Widened Amid the Pandemic." Gallup, December 27, 2021. https://www.gallup.com/workplace/358349/gender-gap-worker-burnout-widened-amid-pandemic.aspx.

48 Gallup. "How to Prevent Employee Burnout." n.d., accessed January 7, 2022. https://www.gallup.com/workplace/313160/preventing-and-dealing-with-employee-burnout.aspx.

49 Project Implicit, "Implicit Association Test (IAT)," n.d., accessed June 3, 2022, https://implicit.harvard.edu/implicit/education.html.